The Act of Being

The Act of Being

Charles Marowitz

Secker & Warburg
London

First published in England 1978 by
Martin Secker & Warburg Limited
54 Poland Street, London W1V 3DF

Copyright © Charles Marowitz 1978

SBN : 436 27326 8

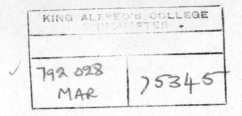

Printed and bound in Great Britain by
Cox & Wyman Limited,
London, Fakenham and Reading

For Julia Leland Crosthwait,

With love . . .

to say the least

Contents

Acknowledgments

"Notes on 'The Theatre of Cruelty' " first appeared in *Theatre at Work*, edited by C. Marowitz and S. Trussler, published by Methuen & Co, London, and Hill and Wang, New York. "*An Othello* Casebook" by John Burgess first appeared in *Theatre Quarterly* No. 8 and is reprinted by permission of TQ Publications, 44 Earlham Street, London WC2.
The Production Memos for Pablo Picasso's *The Four Little Girls* first appeared in the *Tulane Drama Review*.

List of Illustrations

Introduction

There is a presumption in this book which I must own up to at the start.

No one ever taught me how to act or how to direct. Everything in this book is the result of an eclecticism I couldn't begin to index and represents findings derived from a personal, some might say eccentric, approach.

When I was fifteen or sixteen, I went for a few months to a drama school attached to the Henry Street Playhouse on the lower east side of New York. There, a hypnotic young man named Blair Cutting put me in touch with some of the ideas of Michael Chekhov. Being refinements of more basic ideas I had never learned, it all sounded a bit like double-dutch to me. Some light filtered through, but only in uneven shafts like a venetian blind not properly shut.

A year or so later, a lady named Kay Rockefeller allowed me to bore the pants off her in drama-classes at the Young Men's Hebrew

Association on 92nd Street. A teenaged boy with spots and a voice
like a faulty tin-whistle tackling roles like Macbeth rapidly becomes
aware that his acting attributes, compared to, say, Laurence Olivier,
are somewhat impoverished. I was just beginning to ask myself
what I thought I was doing when the question was rather more
forcefully put by my tutors.

When I was eighteen or nineteen, I joined Paul Curtis's American
Mime Theatre where, in jockstrap and loose-fitting leotards, I com-
ported myself in the manner of Marcel Marceau for about a year.

I was unfortunately shaped to be a mime and found myself
successful only when called upon to play grotesques. I developed a
sympathy for grotesques which fortunately stayed with me, as in
later life I became more and more of a grotesque myself. Among
my few "roles", the most memorable was as an illuminated-flipper
in a pin-ball machine, an interpretation so charged with electricity
that subsequently I was immediately thought of whenever anyone
was looking to cast the role of an electron, a valve or a neon-light.
Despite the American Mime Theatre's predisposition to poetry and
metaphysics, Curtis was a disciple of the Method and through him,
I learned the rudiments of the Stanislavsky technique. In my early
twenties, wishing to leave America, I managed, without auditioning,
to obtain a place at the London Academy of Music and Dramatic
Art where it was soon apparent that whatever I was, it wasn't an
actor. I had a strident New York nasality in my voice and a body
shaped like a pretzel. Had I turned up at a House of Correction for
Backward Youths, I would have been accepted without a blink. At
LAMDA, I was more than a fish out of water; I was a pterodactyl
that had flapped in from another age. With a pair of Brillo-like
whiskers precariously poised on a triangularly-set face which resisted
any camouflage, I was probably the most hilarious King John that
ever trod the boards. When I left the Academy, the sigh of relief
was so immense you could have used it to power sailboats up the
Thames.

My experience of British acting techniques collided rudely with
the little knowledge I had acquired in New York, and it soon became
clear to me that neither "school" had the slightest idea of what
acting was all about. Having proved myself a failure at drama
schools both in New York and London, it seemed the most natural
thing in the world to set up an acting-school of my own – if not to

edify others then at least to instruct myself. This was duly estab-lished and when the Method Workshop opened its doors in the late Fifties, I was, on the strength of a few months of Stanislavsky train-ing and a short tour in a mime company, passing myself off as one of America's leading Method exponents.

During the course of the next three years, I felt compelled to produce something of value for actors who were paying me good money, so I started to create for myself an entire body of instruction. I read Stanislavsky, put the few kernels of ideas scrounged from Blair Cutting and Paul Curtis into a mixer and proceeded to discover for myself how, and by what means, Stanislavsky could be applied both to modern works and to classics. During this period, I invented perhaps five hundred improvisations and about a hundred acting-exercises. Ostensibly, I was teaching acting to a group of English professionals; in fact, they were teaching me. I suppose we were teaching each other. The only twinge of guilt was that I was being paid for it whereas, had all things been equal, I should have been paying them. In any case, it was during this period, exploring virgin territory with my own theatrical hymen largely intact, that I started to grasp the intricacies of the art I had begun to profess.

Eventually, in about 1958, I widened my activities and started a theatre-company called In-Stage. In 1968, this became the Open Space Theatre. In the interim, I had joined forces with Peter Brook at the Royal Shakespeare Company and created an experimental group based on the writings and ideas of Antonin Artaud. In the years that followed I organized acting-seminars and professional workshops in Germany, France and Scandinavia. I taught at the Grotowsky Seminar in Holstebro, Denmark, and started a workshop in Heidelberg at which my exercises and techniques were applied to about a hundred professional German actors. Today in London, apart from directing plays commercially and at my own theatre, I conduct acting studios on a fairly regular basis and people offer me preposterous sums to go abroad to spread a gospel which is as sketchy and improvised as this potted history would lead you to believe.

In short, I started as a charlatan, invented my own tuition, put highly personal constructions on to half a dozen half-baked ideas which I'd acquired in New York and London and came up with a *modus operandi* which served my own work but which, quite

possibly, has no application anywhere else. These are my "qualifications". This is the "background" from which this book has been
derived. Anyone desiring something more orthodox or more "legitimate" ought to stop reading right here.

Most acting-books ought to be on the fiction and not on the non-
fiction shelves. Not because they are full of lies, but because they are
full of poetry, mysticism, anecdote and drama. Acting is the kind
of subject that encourages a highly impressionist style of writing.
Rather than talk about what it is, writers tend to describe what it
does.

The general assumption is that once the "rules of acting" are
learned, it can be practised by almost anyone possessing some
modicum of talent. We know, for instance, that actors use words
and so, acting-tuition concentrates on the development of vocal
resonance and projection, on the structure and rendition of language. We also know that it involves physical action, and so it
concerns itself with the actor's body, making sure it is plastic and
serviceable to his will. We know, since Stanislavsky, that it has to
do with inner states, the correct organization of the actor's psychology, and so actors are taught how to conjure up the emotions
appropriate to any given situation. We know that actors simulate
different types of people and so, using a great arsenal of external
aids, everything from humpbacks to stomach-padding, we encourage
them to "observe" life so they can fashion characters with verisimilitude. Brecht persuaded us that the actor also has an obligation to
the social and moral intentions of his characters, and so we accept
that in certain circumstances, choices have to be made which indicate
alternative courses of action. Artaud exhorted actors to grapple with
the tempestuous world of feeling that swirled behind language, and
so exercises and games were devised through which the actor
attempted to make contact with deeper impulses in the theatre.
Acting, bred in rhetoric, refined into naturalism, then realism and
psychological-realism, began to concern itself with metaphysics.

In all of these efforts, the actor's basic abilities, his ability to speak,
to move, to experience and to emote, were harnessed to one technique, now to another. Despite the variations, the basic premise remained the same. The actor was employing his tools (voice, movement, characterization, the outer expression of inner states) in order

to express his material, i.e. the intentions of either the author or the director, latterly the acting-collective. But the basic source from which all these techniques derived their energy was never really analysed – beyond glib admissions that acting had to do with consciousness and subconsciousness, choice and accident, technique and instinct. *Acting* is what actors did. One simply had to observe, acquire a few disciplines and eventually get the hand of it.

In the nineteenth century there was a great concern over whether the actor should lose himself in his role (operate entirely by instinct) or organize his actions under strict conscious control. These were erroneously called different "schools" of acting, and throughout the controversy no one made the elementary point that any acting worth its salt must be composed of both elements, and that even if he wanted to, an actor could not eliminate conscious control, and even if he chose to do so, an actor could not perform entirely on a wave of untrammelled instincts as the result of such performance would be to destroy his coherence and, more likely than not, his sanity. But this controversy (which tends to get revived every fifteen or twenty years) was indirectly concerned with the question I have posed. It wasn't really about how the actor achieves his effects but, unconsciously, about the chemistry of those effects. The preoccupation with methodology obscured that question and, consequently, no strides were made towards answering it. Subsequent works inspired by this dispute only elaborated previously held opinions. Each author found his own way of saying what everyone already believed and stock, unchallenged ideas perpetuated themselves.

The fact is our most influential works on acting are not written by Coquelin or Stanislavsky but by Sigmund Freud, Carl Jung and Alfred Adler. Our acting "theory" is, very largely, extrapolations from our theories of psychology. And if we look at the past twenty years in the theatre, years which have thrown up acting-collectives such as the Living Theatre and the Open Theatre, the laboratories of Jerzy Grotowsky and the experiments of Peter Brook, it becomes clear that the seminal influence on the new acting has not been a book on acting at all, but Antonin Artaud's *The Theatre and its Double*, a rhetorical, almost poetic work of exhortation with no blueprints and almost no didacticism. The work that most influenced acting before that was Gordon Craig's essays *On the Art of the*

Theatre, again a work-of-the-imagination rather than a how-to book. The most influential of all teachers of acting has, of course, always been Aristotle.

Some of the most prevalent acting "theories" consist of nothing more than maxims which contain, in themselves, an entire esthetic philosophy. For some people, "live your part" is just such a maxim. For others, "play it with feeling" is just as edifying. Before we dismiss these words as banalities, it is worth remembering that behind any maxim gainfully employed, lies a vast iceberg of pragmatic theory of which the maxim is only the tip.

Acting is not a science, in so much as it cannot be reduced to formulae or proven by objective criteria. Nor is it, strictly speaking, an art in that it relies upon the artistic creation of others to express itself. And yet we know that it realizes itself most successfully when it is subject to prescribed esthetic conditions and reveals those elements of imagination which we associate with the creation of art. Any desire for certainty is bound to be frustrated. The most we can hope for are partial insights, fugitive perceptions and sporadic glimpses of truth, but the best way to encourage these is to proceed on the assumption that there *is* a foundation of order, even if it can never be satisfactorily verified.

If one attempts to write a book on acting, one should resolve to ground all flights of fancy and to make it as practical as possible. The discursive tendency is almost irresistible, and since acting is compounded from theories of different kinds, it is impossible not to employ speculations, hypotheses and *theories*. And yet, the notion persists that to write a useful book on the subject one must concern oneself with tangible, thoroughly concrete factors. The actor, although vulnerable to theory, practises his art with the use of his body and his voice, his mind and his temperament, and any book which allegedly deals with acting must instruct these things. The challenge, then, is to write something which manages to balance theory and practice and does not dwindle into abstractions and impressions or reduce itself to the level of a training-manual; and, perhaps most important of all, a book that does not sidestep essential questions which do not yield easy and reassuring answers.

I have spelt out the pitfalls as much for myself as for the reader so that when I become discursive or uselessly theoretical, he can tune me out; and when I become too didactic and "technical", he can skip those passages without compunction, remembering my own strictures against them. As for the quest for some essential definition of acting, this may never materialize, although it will be a constant preoccupation in the pages that follow.

1 *Stanislavsky and After*

Since the 1930s, the prevailing doctrines of acting-theory have been derived from the writings and work of Konstantin S. Stanislavsky; most notably from three works published after his death – *An Actor Prepares, Building a Character* and *Creating a Role*. But long before the Thirties when these works first appeared in English, Stanislavsky's influence was permeating the theatre in Europe – most significantly in the work of Jacques Coupeau in France.

In America, in 1905, Alla Nazimova, one of the earliest alumni of the Moscow Arts Theatre, performed Chirikov's *A Chosen People* in Russian in a hall on the lower east side of New York. She later became one of America's leading exponents of Ibsen. In 1922, Richard Boleslavsky, another early member of the Moscow Arts (he was in the First Studio which effectively researched what came to be known as the Stanislavsky System) arrived in America – one year before the visit of the Moscow Arts Company. In 1923, Boleslavsky and Maria Ouspenskaya (who remained in the States after the return of the Russian company) founded the American Lab Theatre. Among its earliest students were Lee Strasberg, Harold Clurman and Stella Adler; all destined to become architects of the Method, the Americanized version of Stanislavsky's basic teaching.

Boleslavsky's influence on Strasberg was seminal, and it is worth remembering that Boleslavsky knew only of Stanislavsky's earliest work – long before the reversals and reappraisals which took place in his last period, in the mid-Thirties. It was from Boleslavsky, whose "theories" were imbued with a kind of spiritual romanticism peculiar to the Twenties, that we first learn the idea of "useless tension"; the existence of that stress which interferes with the free flow of acting-energy. It is from Boleslavsky that we get the homily about "living one's part" instead of adopting outward behaviour to indicate a character's mood or emotions. It is Boleslavsky who makes a fetish of *relaxation* and *concentration* and it is Boleslavsky who introduces us to the concept of Affective Memory, which he borrowed from Ribot, a French psychologist who had originated it forty years before. And it is this same Affective Memory which is soon to become Emotional Memory and the basis for Strasberg's Private Moment exercise.

After the prolix restatements of innumerable revisionists, it is useful to read Boleslavsky on the subject:

> After having decided what feeling is necessary for a certain part of his role, the actor tries to find in his "affective memory", a recollection similar to that particular feeling. He may use all kinds of means in order to bring that feeling to life, starting with the actual lines of the author and finishing with experiences from his own life, recollections from books, and finally using his own imagination. Then, by a series of gradual exercises and rehearsals, he brings himself into a state, enabling him to arouse to the strongest degree, the necessary feeling by a mere thought of it and to retain it for the necessary period of time.

It is from Boleslavsky and the American Lab Theatre (via Stanislavsky with various diversions through Freud and a handful of French psychologists) that the whole notion of inner-technique is, in the early 1920s, unleashed upon an unsuspecting acting profession. Eight years after the commencement of the American Lab

Theatre, Lee Strasberg, training the first company of the Group Theatre, is pounding the imperatives of "true feeling" into a group of American actors which includes Morris Carnovsky, Lee J. Cobb, Clifford Odets, Elia Kazan, Luther and Stella Adler and the other Group pioneers. "Strasberg," Harold Clurman reports in his Thirties memoir *The Fervent Years*, "was a fanatic on the subject of true emotion. Everything was secondary to it. He sought it with the patience of an inquisitor, he was outraged by trick substitutes, and when he had succeeded in stimulating it, he husbanded it, fed it, and protected it. Here was something new to most of the actors, something almost holy. It was revelation in the theatre, and Strasberg was its prophet."

Then in 1934, after six weeks of training with Stanislavsky himself, Stella Adler returned to the Group Theatre to announce to an astonished company, We're doing it all wrong! The Affective Memory exercise was only to be used in very special cases when everything else failed, and was by no means a "tenet" of the System. "Many of the actors from the beginning," writes Stella Adler about this period, "suffered strain, despite the importance of relaxation in an actor's work. To a large degree, this was because the actor was asked, through the use of this 'Affective Memory' or emotional substitution, to deal consciously with that part of himself which was intended to remain unconscious . . . From the beginning, the System benefited chiefly the more experienced actors. They knew they could act – had already done it – had fulfilled the requirements needed in the professional theatre . . . They had the confidence which comes with performance, no matter how critical one is. They used the Method in this context . . . The others, less experienced, less hardy, accepted the new approach literally. A great many of these failed in their development as actors and lost confidence in their old techniques. They became confused."

Among those who presumably "accepted the new approach literally" was Lee Strasberg, who raised Emotional Memory (and its near kin, the Sense-Memory exercise) to the status of a rite. And when corrected by the Master himself via the recently enlightened disciple Stella Adler, Strasberg produced the rationalization that virtually gave birth to the American Method; namely that Stanislavsky had gone back on his own teachings (an understandable misconception since neither Strasberg nor Boleslavsky could be expected to be aware of developments in Russia after 1922) and besides (the other strand in the rationalization), this was Strasberg's "system" not Stanislavsky's. (Although, it would have been more accurate to call it Boleslavsky's.) From that day forward, the Method, derived at second-hand, became the splendidly flawed influence which, it seems to me though it spawned the Brandos, the Steigers, the Wallachs and the Deans, probably crippled ten actors for every one that it aided, and became an artistically prestigious cover for psychotheraphy in a city (and a country) where psycho-neurosis was fashionable, widespread and, outside the confines of the Actor's Studio, expensive.

At this point in time, it seems clear that Emotional Memory, as encouraged by the Studio, is an artificial and disruptive technique which can produce stunning results in the classroom but is chemically unsuited to the needs of performance. No technique which encourages an actor to introduce an emotional non-sequitur into his performance can be anything but misguided. Strasberg's blind spot seems to be that the one thing one never needs to teach an actor is how to feel: if they have any talent for their art at all, it is the one thing that takes care of itself. To be a human being is to experience emotion, and actors already have stored away in their memory cells all the emotions to be summoned up during their work. The problem is often how to escalate a feeling from something small yet distinct into the greater dimensions required by a role. We all know what it is like to want to dominate other people, but that doesn't qualify us to express the enormity of Tamburlaine's ego, and though we have all felt the twinge of pride over accomplishment, it is not quite what is needed to sustain Coriolanus for over three hours. The problem is not evoking emotions but enlarging them to meet the demands of demanding material – i.e. classical and epic texts rather than psychologically realistic chamber-plays. Eugene Vakhtangov, Stanislavsky's most brilliant student, reminds us of Stanislavsky's own priorities in this extract from his diary:

Critics of Stanislavsky's doctrines often overlook the statement which takes first place in the system and methods of Stanislavsky: That the actor should not be concerned about his feeling during a play, it will come of itself. They label as auto-suggestion and narcotic self-intoxication the help which Stanislavsky gives to students in recalling their intimate experience. But Stanislavsky maintained the opposite: don't try to experience, don't make feelings to order, forget about them altogether. In life, our feelings come to us by themselves against our will. Our willing gives birth to action directed towards the gratification of desire. If we succeed in gratifying it, a positive feeling is born spontaneously. If an obstacle stands in the way of gratifying it, a negative feeling is born, viz. "suffering". An action directed towards the gratification of will is continuously accompanied by a series of spontaneous feelings, the content of which is the anticipation of the coming gratification or the fear of failure.

Thus every feeling represents a gratified or non-gratified will. At first, a desire arises that becomes the will, then begins to act consciously, aiming towards its gratification. Only then, altogether spontaneously, and sometimes against our will, does the feeling come. Thus, feeling is a product of will and the conscious (and sometimes subconscious) actions directed towards its gratification.

Therefore, the actor, Stanislavsky taught, must think first of all about what he wants to obtain at a particular moment and what he is to do, but not about what he is going to feel.

This is the classical Stanislavsky dictum about the urge to action; the need to discover the mainspring of action in a character's behaviour as made apparent by the text. It is the most profound of Stanislavsky's discoveries and the most practical aspect of the Method in so much as it by-passes all the convoluted nonsense about *really* feeling or *simulating* feeling or acquiring some highly rationalized balance between the two. It is the quintessential impulse behind all acting: the will to do, the drive to want, the urge to act. And it is the biological opposite of engendering emotion for its own sake in order to apply it where it may be wanting in a scene. This is like asking the painter to spend his most creative efforts in elaborately mixing paints on the assumption that, at some point, what he has concocted will be able to be used in the creation of a work of art; instead of exhorting him to express himself using the paint already at his disposal.

The other great flaw in Strasberg's curiously attenuated Method approach is the equation between the actor's and the character's psyche. It is part of the accepted ideology of the Studio to believe that the basis for any character-building is the actor's personal mode of behaviour. It is *your* vacillation that feeds Hamlet, your ambition that permeates Macbeth, your temperamental fragility that brings about the downfall of Blanche du Bois. In one sense, this is unassailable. The actor has only himself at his disposal. He can work only with *his* emotions, *his* temperament, *his* store of memories. Should he fail to work with himself, he is in danger of imitating or faking so, of course, he must return constantly to his own well-springs. But if the character he is portraying contains an intensity of feeling beyond his emotional scope, he must, of necessity, transcend his personal limitations; he must fill out the contours of those characters more imaginatively conceived than himself.

How often has one heard the criticism that Method actors always play themselves? In one sense, this is unwarranted – as all they *have* is themselves and the real sin is not so much playing oneself but not having enough of oneself to play. But the criticism has validity when pint-size actors relying on a woefully inadequate emotional range attempt to create characters that require greater endowments than they can provide. It is then that the Method is seen to be a diminution rather than a realization of acting possibilities. This fault is compounded by the Method actor who, with practised indulgence, has been taught that *his* feelings, and *his* character is precisely what the contemporary theatre demands – without ever scrutinizing the scope of those feelings nor the breadth of that character. Here the old truism, there is no such thing as small roles, only small actors, applies. Small actors can make small characters out of large ones, small plays out of great ones. Any theory that persuades an actor that the sincerity of his feeling and the truthfulness of his actions are all that is required in the creation of art misunderstands esthetics as much as it over-prizes individuality. The emphasis on truth which permeates every page that Stanislavsky ever wrote is a staple of all art. Truth is the lifeblood of art but, to serve a useful purpose, it has to pump itself into a great number of vital organs and they, in turn, have to be served by muscles and nerves that enable the organism to function. By stressing inner truthfulness at the expense of other equally relevant, and often more unobtainable, virtues, the Method creates an artificial ethic which tends to encourage mediocrity.

It is significant that the Method appears to have little truck with writers such as Beckett, Ionesco, Genet, and Arrabal, or that a gifted director such as Elia Kazan suddenly finds his considerable expertise frustrated by a work like *The Changeling*, or that almost every Method-trained director finds it necessary to modify or abandon his approach in the face of writers such as Shakespeare and Marlowe. And it is equally significant that traditional British acting, ostensibly preoccupied with externals and eschewing the complexities of inner technique, should be more successful with the works of all the aforementioned writers.

Before passing on, we should pause to explode the fallacy that the British actor is some kind of living advertisement to speech-training and physical deportment with none of the resources usually associated with the Stanislavsky-trained actor. This has always been rubbish even when the British actor has believed it himself, and proceeded to defend himself against the charge. The best actors no matter what their "school" have been united by a manifestation of talent that transcends any methodology or arbitrary classification. A list of actors epitomizing Stanislavskian virtues, that is, actors possessing an untrammelled instinct, unquestioned credibility, emotional power and communicated-sensitivity, would contain names such as Laurence Olivier, Ralph Richardson, Trevor Howard, Charles Laughton, Robert Newton, Alan Badel, Paul Scofield, Nicol Williamson – none of whom would acknowledge any particular debt to Stanislavsky. The English actor is not constitutionally external; he is simply, by training and culture, a more finished social product. He possesses a more positive speaking voice; he overcomes his diffidence or insecurity with a more pronounced physical presence. His "assurance" is based on the dimly perceived fact that he has behind him ten centuries of social and political history, and four centuries of unparalleled cultural achievement. No wonder he speaks well, moves with authority and cuts a fine figure. No wonder, too, that he tends to rely on his external attributes and distrusts long-haired analytical probings from foreign sources. Did they ever improve Kean or Forbes Robertson? Mrs Fiske or Ellen Terry? Do they add anything to the magnetism of Olivier or Richardson, Finney or O'Toole? These often unspoken reservations fortify the British actors' resistance to Method incursions. But it would be foolish to deduce that the virtues of this approach are absent simply because the principles are not subscribed to. How could one reconcile such a belief with the fact that the English actor is the recipient of universal approbation and, in America alone, is looked up to as an exemplar of his art.

The English actor, adhering to Vakhtangov's dictum via Stanislavsky (neither of whose theories he has ever heard) does not preoccupy himself with emotional theories, he just acts, and if he is lucky (i.e. talented) the emotion takes care of itself. If he is unlucky (i.e. run-of-the-mill), he personifies that combination of emotional vacuum and external overlay which has been representative of English acting for over two hundred years – for the curious fact is that the great English actors have always been the splendid exceptions, the mediocre actor, the general rule. In America, there are not many outstanding performers – not to compare with Olivier and Richardson, Gielgud and Scofield – but the average American actor has always been head-and-shoulders above his British counterpart, for what systematic training *can* do is to develop the existing skills that actors do possess – whereas an English mediocrity with no recourse to Method correctives, remains a mediocrity to the end of his days.

But to return to the Method . . . It seems to me that there is a connection between the dearth of modern American playwriting and the predominance of an acting-style which has effectively precluded any work other than examples of psychologically realistic drama. (Oddities like the Living Theatre and the Open Theatre, Happenings and the work of Robert Wilson emerge like fascinating pimples which suggest some fundamental imbalance in the bloodstream of drama.) Year after year, season after season, the "new writing" consists of anaemic re-hashes of work influenced by the American Titans – Eugene O'Neill, Arthur Miller and Tennessee Williams (which is perhaps why the appearance of mutations such as Sam Shepard or Michael McClure creates so much initial enthusiasm as the assembly-line is more regularly concerned with the production of neo-realists such as John Ford Noonan, John Guare, Preston Jones and David Rabe).

Could it be that the limitations imposed by the Method actually discourage the creation of any literary style not susceptible to psychologically realistic treatment? Is it possible that the American writer produces only what he knows the American actor can do and the American public will accept? Is it possible that almost every new

American play is only some elaborately extended version of Strasberg's Private Moment exercise; a reconstruction of manageable
emotional memories compounded in the form of a social or political
"problem play" which the American actor can "get his teeth into"
simply because it is matter already swilling around in his mouth? Is
this the reason why, perhaps, the imported English drama is so
successful; the reason why a Tom Stoppard (a writer in whom the
stilted two-step of naturalism and psychology is banished in favour
of a bold artifice of language), comes as such a revelation? And is
it also why, perhaps, Americans regularly embrace the visits of the
Royal Shakespeare Company? For if classics are anything they are
the triumph of form and content over the mundane trivia of tele-
visual soap-opera tarted up as "serious drama" and populated with
"people just like you and I".

Before I leave the impression that I am laying the whole of
America's theatrical problems at the threshold of the Actor's Studio,
I had better say that although there is no identifiable single cause,
there is an obvious connection between the American theatre's obses-
sion with social verisimilitude and the Method's preoccupation with
psychological realism. In the case of both, there is a reduction of the
theatre's possibilities, a reliance on known quantities and identifiable types. And if we forsake the larger generality for the moment
(the American drama) and concentrate only on the subject that
pertains to this treatise, American acting, we see that the principles
of the Method, as applied at the Studio, help to encourage an in-
ward-looking, border-narrowing, rather than horizon-widening,
outlook. Not only does it stimulate reproductions of itself, it tends
to accept that the psychological density of any situation is as far as
one need look; as if all behaviour verified by Freudian postulates is
verified entirely and for all time. Without meaning to do so, it foists
a simplistic view of life, and one that can be mechanically interpreted according to given formulae. It's as if as soon as you have
discovered Hamlet's super-objective and the sequence of actions
that constitute his progress in the play, there is nothing more to be
said – either about the character or the work. It denies the existence
of dimensions which cannot be reduced to Method terminology and
makes no provisions for unverifiable phenomena like surrealism,
fantasy, magic and that flouter of all conventions, genius. It is a safe
technology for actors committed to safe travel and although it can

be relied on to get you from Point A to Point B, it doesn't always insure that you will experience all the landscape and natural phenomena that abound between those two points. And finally, it is, in contemporary American practice, a renunciation of what Stanislavsky intended it to be – which was not a rigid system of applied esthetic technology but more like a helpful, rather casual guide who says: Why don't you try going down this road, it may get you to your destination? On the other hand, should you decide to turn off at any point along the way, by all means do so – for there is territory down there that even I have never seen and you may find things for yourself every bit as interesting as anything I might suggest.

As to Strasberg himself, my suspicions about the ultimate usefulness of his teaching stem initially from the fact that he is not a successful theatre director. Theoretically, any man guiding the steps of actors must be accountable for the performances they give – particularly those under his own direction. Apart from one or two lukewarm productions in the early days of the Group Theatre, Strasberg has not been particularly successful as a stage director. His own Method-dominated production of Chekhov's *The Three Sisters* was to my mind lamentable as a production and infuriating as a misapplication of Stanislavsky techniques.

One casts these doubts on Strasberg to try to reconcile his counterproductive practices as an acting-teacher with his immense reputation, and my conclusion is that one has no real bearing on the other. Whatever status he may have as an American personality, his application of Stanislavsky technique, as acquired from Boleslavsky, is in my view a detrimental influence on modern American acting.

It is significant to note the differences between Strasberg and his great mentor. Stanislavsky was a proven actor and an indisputably and outstandingly successful director. He encouraged his disciples (Vakhtangov, Meyerhold, Tairov, etc.) to go off and create their own styles and their own theatres. He was deeply concerned with the development of the young actor, but personally took no hand in the publication of his acting treatises. In a word, he had nothing to prove; he was already a proven quantity. Strasberg, on the other hand, had constantly to prove himself in the Group Theatre – particularly after his teaching was questioned by Stella Adler, and afterwards, when his own credibility as a director had been undermined by several failures. And although it is possible to take a career as a less than successful director and convert it into one as a successful teacher, there is an interconnection between acting and direction which makes it impossible to assess the values of one without relating them to the practice of the others.

The student–teacher relationship, we know, is as all-engulfing as that of the analyst and the analysand. The student's reliance on the teacher is often total. All forms of approval or disapproval emanate from the teacher and either strengthen or weaken the confidence of the student. If the subject of study is "specialized", that is if there is a presumption of mystery about it, arcane knowledge which can only be loosed from the guru to the disciple, then the student's reliance is even greater. It develops an almost religious significance; acting becomes like the taking of holy orders; the teacher, a high priest – and this is so often the way Strasberg is described in relation to the Method, even by his colleague Harold Clurman referring to the earliest days of the Group Theatre. When a discipline graduates into mysticism, it loses the democratic give and take, the necessity to maintain checks and balances, which is invaluable in any intellectual pursuit. It is this possibility of dissent, this need constantly to prove itself, that keeps it up to scratch and prevents a body of living ideas from becoming an empty creed.

In my view the unhealthiest aspect of the Method as practised in New York circles is its totalitarianism. Over the years, it has developed answers to every objection and formulae for the solution of every problem. Within its tightly prescribed limits, it has become entirely self-sufficient. Like Marxism or orthodox Christianity, it can disarm all criticism by reference to its own holy writ. No longer a theory derived from a larger art form (which, in fact, is its historical origin – from actors like Shchepkin, Salvini, and Medvedeva to an observing Stanislavsky), it has become an artistic end in itself. To be "Method" has become a higher goal than to be good.

I do not want to infer by this criticism that there is something fundamentally flawed about the Method. The Method has proved itself over and over again – not only in the early days of the Studio but with dozens of first-class Method teachers such as Herbert Berghof, Uta Hagen and Gene Frankel. As for Strasberg, what I am saying is that, although eminently knowledgeable on the subject of acting, his emphasis on the veracity of feeling is, at base, the result of a rationalization of Stanislavsky's teaching and not the most

useful aspect of those theories now clustered around that wide body
of practice known as the Method. Also, that there is a great danger
in laboratory-work that does not prove itself in practical tests. The
value of a Method exercise is not its efficacy in the classroom but its
benefit to a performance, and that equation – classroom-findings
applied to practical-work – is not made at the Studio; and when it
is, artificial criteria fostered by the Studio situation itself tend to be
applied. By such measuring rods, it is possible to earn approbation
simply because Method practitioners and their cult public all know
and share the same rules of procedure, whereas for the uninitiated
there is only murky subjectivity and self-indulgence.

What is significant about Stanislavsky's principles is that they
need not be circumscribed by Method practice. They can, in fact, be
widened out to serve a very different kind of theatrical work. I have
found the Method a useful foundation for the almost antithetical
ideas of Antonin Artaud.

STANISLAVSKY AND ARTAUD

Having been brought up on Stanislavsky and the idea of inner truth,
it was a major adjustment to discover there was also *surface truth*,
and that in certain contexts, the latter was more persuasive than the
former. An even more difficult adjustment was to realize that artifice
and downright artistic fraud could create a plenitude of truth for an
audience and was therefore, according to the pragmatic laws that
govern acting, legitimate. The Method argument for inner truth
holds water only if its main contention is true : that is, that the
spectator experiences feeling to the same degree the actor does. But
we all know this not always the case; that there are hundreds of
instances of turned-on actors splitting themselves with inner intensity communicating nothing to an audience but effort and tension. It
is equally true that an actor who is almost totally turned-off but going
through the right motions in the right context can powerfully affect
an audience – almost involuntarily.

The Method actor's test for truthfulness is the intensity and
authenticity of his personal feeling. The Artaudian actor knows that
unless that feeling has been shaped into a communicative image, it
is a passionate letter without postage. Whereas pure feeling can be
mawkish or leaden, a pertinent stage-image – a gesture, a movement,
a sequence of actions – is a statement in itself which doesn't require

the motor-power of feeling in order to register, but when emotionally charged is many times more potent.

There is no fundamental disagreement between the Method actor
and the Artaudian actor. Both rely on consciousness to release the
unconscious, but whereas the Method actor is chained to rational
motivation, the Artaudian actor realizes the highest artistic truth is
unprovable. Like certain rare natural phenomena that defy scientific
analysis, they *can* exist – and the actor's task is to conjure them into
being.

The Artaudian actor needs Stanislavsky in order to verify the
nature of the feelings he is releasing – otherwise he becomes merely
a victim of feeling. Even Artaud's celebrated actor-in-trance is responsible to the spirit that is speaking through him. A séance where
nothing is communicated but atmosphere is not half as rewarding
as one in which messages are received loud and clear. The very state
of trance itself is arrived at methodically. The medium's secret is
knowing when to let go of the mechanisms that have produced it, in
order to transcend them; the same is true for the actor – any actor –
who uses either intellect or instinct to bring him to a crucial
jumping-off point.

The stage we have reached today is that Stanislavsky's ideas are
no longer being extended and researched. They are being solidified
by one "school" or another. As Strasberg himself pointed out in
1947, the underlying point of the System was not to systematize,
"not to play this or that part but how to act organically". It was as a
creative formula that Stanislavsky's ideas spawned the very different
theatres of Meyerhold and Vakhtangov, and it is as a creative formula that it can be used today to create styles and techniques which
will transcend the narrow limits of room-size realism.

If one were able to cut through the flak of New York Method
practices, past the febrile explorations of The Group Theatre and
the oversimplifications of people like Boleslavsky and Bulgakov;
if one were able to return to the subsoil of Stanislavsky's own thinking, one would get from the theories what is most valuable and most
rare – the stimulus to develop new and expanded ideas to serve the
needs of the twentieth-century theatre which, still hung over with
nineteenth-century moss and algae, is nevertheless dredging itself
into the twenty-first century.

POSTSCRIPT

When the Moscow Arts Theatre Company came to London in the early
Sixties, I had an opportunity to talk to its Artistic Director about the
matters which pertain to some of the matters just discussed. I insert here,
as an addendum, excerpts from an article written at that time.

As one viewed *Cherry Orchard*, *Three Sisters* and *Uncle Vanya* one
became increasingly aware of a kind of grand manner attack which I
could only call "theatrical". This panache may be a strictly Russian
characteristic but I doubt it. Reviewers praised the company for giving
London "the real Chekhov" but at the same time it intruded that turn-
of-the-century *schmaltz* that Chekhov, and Stanislavsky, were opposed
to but which Stanislavsky could no sooner keep out of his production
than Chekhov could keep it out of his plays . . .

My curiosity about the company stemmed from the fact that what I
was seeing was a group, several generations removed from the Moscow
Arts Theatre celebrated in the Twenties and Thirties. I was eager to
see just how it had altered since those pioneer days of the revolution,
and exactly what went on inside. The man to give me this information
was Victor J. Stanitsyn, the Art Director of the theatre, and the man
who, under the new dispensation, most closely filled Stanislavsky's
shoes.

A massive, delicately spectacled Russian who inhabits rather than
wears his tasteful European clothes, Stanitsyn has been with the
Moscow Arts Theatre since 1918. After four years of training in the
Moscow Arts school, he graduated into the company as an actor, but
his inclination was towards direction. To demonstrate his abilities, he
rehearsed Dickens's *Pickwick Club* with junior members of the
company and presented it before Stanislavsky. The Maestro saw and
approved it, and Stanitsyn became one of the youngest directors in the
MAT.

During his early tenure as an actor, Stanitsyn, under the direction of
Stanislavsky, was playing the role Ivan the Fool in a fairy tale by
Tolstoy. A rather stolid, serious type even then, Stanitsyn couldn't
muster up the necessary naïveté the role demanded. Stanislavsky
invited him to his house for extra rehearsals. When he arrived, he
found the tall, owl-faced producer in the midst of dozens of toys.
Stanislavsky motioned Stanitsyn to join him on the floor, and the wary
Stanitsyn sat himself down wondering what aspect of the System all
this was supposed to illustrate. All of Stanitsyn's formal requests to

commence work on the play were subtly dismissed as Stanislavsky continued to manipulate the toys and urge Stanitsyn to do the same. Feeling one had to humour the great man's whims, Stanitsyn began toying with the objects. Before long, the wheeled, sprung, tooting, snapping toys inspired a genuine fascination and the two men became heartily engrossed in childsplay. "There," Stanislavsky suddenly called out, "now you've got it! That's what Ivan is like. Just like that!"

Although an avowed acting-disciple of Stanislavsky, Stanitsyn feels his knowledge of stagecraft and direction accrues mostly from Nemirovitch-Danchenko, the co-founder of the MAT and a gentleman usually neglected when the theatre is discussed in the West. Stanitsyn tries to remain true to Nemirovitch-Danchenko's production credo: "When the curtain rises and the actors come to life, the director must die!" The credo was well-demonstrated in Stanitsyn's production of *The Cherry Orchard*. The director's hand was nowhere visible; one felt only the impact of the acting he had evoked . . .

The Stanislavsky System has become second nature in Russia. It dominates all drama training throughout the country. But I discovered that its interpretation is by no means doctrinaire. "Stanislavsky, in our country," says Stanitsyn, "is not a monument, but a pattern. Each director makes his own contributions to the system and adjusts and rearranges it according to his own lights." When questioned about the use of sense-memory, Stanitsyn had to think a long while before he realized what I was referring to. "That too," he said, "actors use according to whether or not they find it personally effective." The endless readings, so notorious in the early days of the Moscow Arts, have apparently been greatly reduced. "We read each act two or three times and then begin to act it." However, as Stanitsyn went on to explain, that doesn't mean it goes from the table to the stage. Before embarking on moves, there are exploratory rehearsals during which actors, in an attempt to establish contact with one another and unravel the intent of the dialogue, simply face each other and run through the play's text. Once contact has been established and there is agreement on the playwright's meaning, the blocking* is begun.

The low-frequency attack (popularized by the Actor's Studio) which results in a good deal of initial muttering and mumbling has apparently been done away with. According to Stanitsyn, Stanislavsky himself renounced his early overemphasis on "inner feelings" because they bottled up the actor's real energy. Today in the Moscow Arts,

* Blocking is the American term for staging.

actors are encouraged to attack their roles with an uninhibited gusto, the assumption being it is better to have to tone down a performance than try to escalate it from a muttering, subjective nothingness. Since Stanislavsky appreciated the value of "overacting" in the pursuit of real feeling, this reversal of the System seems quite credible. Which led me to the question of "real feeling", the avowed end of the System.

"Are the tears real?" I asked Stanitsyn, referring to the innumerable lachrymose outbursts one found in the Chekhov performances. "In almost all cases they are," he explained. "And if an actor has got to reach a high emotional climax and just does not feel it, what does he do?" I asked. "He relies on technique," Stanitsyn answered, "but the technique of our performers is so good that when a performer reaches such a climax, he is *really* there and he doesn't have to fall back on indications."

The Chekhovian performances tended to bear out Stanitsyn's words. One was never aware of the actor arranging technical expedients; the acting flow was organic, and there was a sense of involvement between players that is unknown on the West End stage. The effect was of a realism that never for a moment became suspect. And I am not referring to the studied naturalistic minutiae that a realistic production is usually burdened with. Here, it was, as Stanislavsky had asked it to be, an inner realism; an all-prevailing artistic realism that rendered every move and gesture inevitable. One never praised the significant bit-of-business; one was too busy responding to it. This realistic concept was fortified in a thousand little places. The off-stage party scenes in Stanitsyn's *Cherry Orchard* (visible in this production) were meticulously rehearsed. The rainstorm in Act Three of *Uncle Vanya* was so delicately orchestrated one got an image of the sound-man reading from a score. All lighting was what the time of day compelled it to be; there was almost no atmospheric (mood) lighting. Costume and prop accuracy was historically exact.

"But is this the same Chekhov the audiences of Moscow saw at the turn of the century? Has the interpretation changed?" I asked Stanitsyn. In reply he broke into Gayev's opening speeches in *Cherry Orchard*. With a mournful, wanly nostalgic face and a drooping, tired voice, he reminisced about the "old days" and how times had changed. Then he burst into the same speech with a nervous, agitated attack, almost dismissing the "old days" as pointless, and emphasizing the harshness of the change. "You see," Stanitsyn pointed out, "when Chekhov was first presented, the parts were played by middle-aged or old actors. Today, we have younger people in the casts and that accounts for a lot of the difference in interpretation."

And what of the Western theatre, I asked. "What would you say was the chief difference between the Russian theatre and the English theatre, for instance?"

"In England," Stanitsyn began carefully trying to condense his thought, "an audience receives the impact of a play through the tangibles of its production. In Russia, a play is expressed almost exclusively through its acting." On his visits to London, Stanitsyn had seen only *My Fair Lady* and though he admired its music, he regretted the confusion of differing styles. Did he like the American playwrights? He much enjoyed Lillian Hellman's *Autumn Garden* which was a big success in Moscow, and was looking forward to Arthur Miller's *Death of a Salesman* which the Moscow Arts was now readying for production. And what of the American Method, Elia Kazan, the Actor's Studio? Alas, he had heard very little about it. Our interview ended on a note of astonishment that drove home the remoteness of Moscow from Broadway when to my question, did he admire Marlon Brando, he unblinkingly confessed: "I'm afraid I never heard of him."

2 *Definition of an Actor*

An actor is someone who remembers.

On the simplest level, someone who remembers his lines, his cues, his moves, his notes, to do up his fly-buttons, to tie his shoe-laces, to carry his props, to enter, to exit. Simple things, complex things. An actor is someone who remembers.

On another level, an actor is someone who remembers what it felt like to be spurned, to be proud, to be angry, to be tender – all the manifestations of emotion he experienced as a child, as an adolescent, in early manhood and maturity. An actor remembers the "feel" of all the feelings he ever felt or ever sensed in others. He remembers what happened to other people through all periods of recorded time – through what he has read and been taught. In tracing the lineaments of his own sensibility, he has the key to understanding everyone else.

On a deeper level, an actor is someone who remembers the primitive primordial impulses that inhabited his body before he was "civilized" and "educated". He remembers what it feels like to experience intense hunger and profound thirst, irrational loathing and sublime contentment. He recalls the earliest sensations of light and heat, the invasion of infernal forces and the coming of celestial light. He remembers the anguish of disapproval and the comforting security of guardians.

He remembers vividly (not necessarly articulately) what it feels like to be isolated, to be partnered, to be set adrift, to be reclaimed. He remembers that miasmic stretch of time before becoming aware of the details of his own identity. He remembers the world before it became *his* world and himself before he became his self.

To be without memory and to be an actor is inconceivable. An actor is someone who remembers.

3 A Simplified Method

In the course of the following pages, various terms relating to acting, specifically to techniques based on the work of Stanislavsky, will be freely employed. Despite the mystique which surrounds the subject, the Stanislavsky System-cum-Method can be reduced to about four or five essential ingredients, and by defining a few simple terms, I believe the gist of the theory can become easily accessible to the reader not already familiar with it. All interpretations of Stanislavsky are somewhat personalized and, although the following is fairly standardized stuff, one or two things may appear idiosyncratic to the doctrinaire mind.

PLAYING THE ACTION

An "action" refers to what a character wants. Not what he says he wants, but what his underlying drive compels him towards from moment to moment. This "want" is constantly changing as a result of pressure from other characters with other "wants" (counteractions) and it is the inter-action between the character's actions and the actions of others which produces the conflicts in scenes or, as is sometimes the case, within the character himself.

If I want to leave the room (which is my action) and you wish to prevent me (which is *your* action or the scene's counteraction), the playing-out of our respective actions produces a conflict. If I decide to remain in order to change your mind, I have altered my action. If you then refuse to have your mind changed but instead try to make me feel guilty for wanting to leave in the first place, you have altered your action and are then playing a new counteraction (i.e. counter to my action of trying to change your mind). If I am made to feel guilty and, as a result, try to make you feel *just* as guilty, my action has changed yet again. If you resent being made to feel guilty and try to force me to admit that I am devious and trying to avoid my own guilt by projecting it on to you, you are changing your action once again and playing a new counteraction (i.e. trying to force me to admit my deviousness). If I resent the pressure you are applying and try to make you come to terms with the fact that you are, and always have been, a bully, my action, compelled by your counteraction, changes again (i.e. to make you face up to the fact you are a bully). If this provokes you to the point where you strike me to the ground, your counteraction resolves itself in a physical action. If, being struck, I pretend to be more hurt than I really am in order to make you feel as guilt-ridden as possible, I adopt one of your previous actions and may play it until the end of the scene, or until such time as I feel the force of another counteraction which impels me into yet another action, etc. etc., and so forth.

BEATS

During those moments when any one of my actions is being played against one of your counteractions, we can be said to be in a beat; a section of time confined to a specific set of continuous actions, or perhaps the duration of a mood or an internal state. As soon as our actions graduate to the next unit of activity, we can be said to be in the next beat of the scene. Some beats last for moments. Some go on for entire scenes. A beat, in our usage, is a unit of time bounded by a common preoccupation with related actions. It is characterized by

one overriding emotional colour and distinguishes itself from units
of action which come before and after it.

ACTIVITIES

An activity, unlike an action, is what an actor involves himself with
physically. Through the playing of an activity (reading, cutting his
fingernails, getting dressed, whetting a knife), the action, or underlying aim of the character, should clarify itself. Activities are divided
into primary and secondary. Primary activities refer to physical
actions which entirely preoccupy the character, i.e. fencing, fighting,
making love, etc. Secondary activities are physical actions chosen to
support other, more pressing occupations (i.e. toying with a pen
while dismissing an employee, mixing drinks while seducing a
woman, strumming a guitar while arranging a murder, etc.).

SUB-TEXT

In the course of playing our actions, we are not necessarily revealing
our inner intentions in words. More often, we are concealing them.
So that, for instance, when you are trying to make me feel guilty,
you are not saying, "I am trying to make you feel guilty", but, perhaps, talking about how unhappy my wife is because she has heard
I have been playing around with my secretary. The gist of your
speech may appear to be solicitous and kind. You may be pretending
to be concerned about the survival of my marriage and the importance of honesty in human relations, but your sub-text would be to
make me feel guilty.

The sub-text refers to the character's actual and underlying intent
which conditions his top-text but almost never reveals itself expli-
citly. However, it is this sub-textual intention to which the actor is
essentially connected. It is very rarely made apparent by the playwright. It has to be discovered by the actor. Often, there is a choice
of several sub-textual intentions. The one chosen by the actor,
according to his conception of character, is what ultimately determines interpretation. In substantial works, the choice of sub-text can
be immensely wide and hence the possibility of innumerable interpretations. Take *Hamlet* for instance, in Act I Scene 2, the scene in
which Claudius addresses the Court for the first time as King. For
a good deal of the time, Hamlet is just seated while court business

is being carried on, but depending on his action, the sub-text can have any number of different complexions. His action might be to make Claudius uneasy, to make him as conscious as possible of the moral implications of the act he is performing. Or, he may simply want to disappear, to absent himself from the proceedings because he finds them so painful. Or, the object of his sub-text may be Gertrude; he may, by keeping his gaze fixed on her, try to make her feel as uncomfortable as possible. Or, he may wish to try to subvert the entire ceremony. He may sit in such a way and exude such an air as to suggest dumb insolence to everything and everyone. Or, realizing he is in the act of being usurped by Claudius, he may be frightened for his life; he may sit formal and tense, just hoping he will survive long enough to leave the court safely. Or, he may choose to view the entire ceremony as an indictment against the court of Elsinore which can allow such heinous acts to take place; in which case his focus, throughout the scene, may be out front, on the members of the court watching, listening and making grim silent judgments while the incestuous King consolidates the power to which he is not truly entitled.

In the choice of each action, a new attitude is unleashed; a new mood pervades, a different sub-text obtains.

PLAYING RESULTS

Let us assume I wish to leave a strange room in which I suddenly have found myself. I go to the door and find it is locked. I try to nudge it with my shoulder, but it will not budge. I go to the back-door. I find that too is locked. I move to the window and attempt to open it. I find it firmly locked from the outside and suddenly realize it is also barred. I notice a transom in the ceiling and try to get to it by standing on a chair, but find it far beyond my reach. I go to the walls and beat them with my fist, but they are solid concrete and I realize that no sound can penetrate them. I go to the door again and try kicking it, but to no avail. I go again to the window to try to smash the glass, but find it is too thick even to dent. I jump up to try to reach the transom but all in vain. I rush again to the door and kick it even harder; to the window, beating against the glass; to the back-door, still implacably shut tight.

Result: I am frightened.

Imagine now, that instead of actually going through all the physical actions previously described, I tear my hair, chew my fingernails, roll my eyes, bite my lips, shriek and carry on. I am "showing" fright. I am playing a result rather than a series of actions which produce that result.

A "result" in our terms, is the demonstration of an emotional state rather than the organic feeling brought about by the appropriate performance of actions. It is the inevitable consequence of *indicating* rather than experiencing the "want" that produces the feeling.

INDICATION

Strictly speaking, an actor cannot play fear, joy, suspicion, love, hate, etc. He *can* "indicate" these emotions – that is, by using an appropriate sign-language, he can convey dramatic information to spectators suggesting these states. But when he does this, he is forced to resort to clichés. To avoid clichés, to experience these feelings organically, he must perform actions which will naturally produce them and, because they are real for him, they will have a greater plausibility for an audience.

Of course it is possible for them to be "real" for him and still not communicate to an audience but generally speaking, which is all we are doing at the moment, it is preferable for the actor to put himself (personally) in touch with the feeling he is wanting to convey rather than relying on the "indication" which must encourage him into "results" instead of generating the palpable "sub-text" in any particular "beat" by properly "playing the action".

4 The Morality of Real Life

Art is an abstraction of reality. But what is reality?

A book on acting is certainly not going to answer a question which has defied philosophers and scientists for ages, but within our limited frame of reference, we can accept that for actors, "reality" corresponds to the inner experience and outward behaviour of the world around us. But that doesn't get us anywhere either, since the internal experience and the external appearance of that world differs vastly from one person to another. And yet, even after we acknowledge these differences, and even after we admit there can be no ultimate verification of reality, we must concede that a criterion is still applied. In all our work, and in the language we use in performing it, we constantly relate to some shared concept we call *real life*.

To the actor, *real life* is the accumulation of his own experience and observation. When he says a character's behaviour is not *real*, he means it doesn't correspond to *his* experience of reality. When a director contradicts him and says that for him, a particular piece of behaviour *is* real, it means it confirms a different conception of reality. One would think that the author's conception of reality, as objectified in his play, would settle the matter since it is *his* conception which is being interpreted. And yet it is precisely because interpretation allows lee-way to both the actor and the director that the dispute arises in the first place. So a situation exists in which three persons' conception of reality are all at odds and, presumably, even more conflicting views could be added if other people were coaxed into the controversy.

The only thing this proves conclusively is that any reference to *real life* is a reference to an indefinable ambiguity which can never be satisfactorily nailed down. And yet, despite disputes and disagreements, plays are performed and audiences (which reflect just as many different conceptions as are to be found among artists), generally speaking, accept certain modes of behaviour and, generally speaking, reject others. Some criterion of plausibility gets applied and ultimately, enforced.

I have plodded through these elementary considerations in order to suggest that the imposition of a criterion like *real life* is largely meaningless. No arguments can be won by an actor insisting that a character would not be such-and-such because it isn't like *real life*, and since there can never be a completely shared agreement about what is *real*, one has to avoid the useless clatter of semantic confusions stemming from experimental differences, and try to apply some more sensible, and more generally acceptable criteria.

We may never agree as to what is real when the realities being compared emanate from our own *real lives*, but there is some measure of agreement on which we can agree when the dispute involves style. We do feel (although we cannot necessarily elucidate why) that something-or-other is *out-of-keeping* with the developing style of a scene. Some esthetic warning-siren screeches in our ears when a move or an action goes against the grain of what we are carefully putting together. Something is *out-of-keeping*, something *doesn't belong*, and it suddenly makes us stop in our tracks and eliminate the transgression before we can go on to what is *in keeping* and what *does belong*. This instinct is bred by the material itself – just as the reality of what we are doing is conditioned and contained by that material. Although there may not be a generally held conception that we would all pledge allegiance to as *the truth*, there is some commonly experienced continuum in a work of art which we are prepared to accept as *its* truth. A truth nurtured in a very special way by the material and *its* conceptions which, if they are consistent, persuades us to accept, even if only temporarily, someone else's coherent view of life.

In rehearsals, in order to ascertain the truth of any given moment, the actor and the director have to accept the arbitrary truth of their play and adapt themselves accordingly. In so doing, there is a danger that what an actor finds *uncomfortable* or *strange* may simply be the collision of his own world-view with that of the author's. A value which he does not share may permeate a piece of material in such a way that it discommodes his own value system – in which case the problem is in himself and not his material.

A common example of this occurs when there are differing views on morality. Often an actress is asked to portray a character who is loose and licentious; often, this kind of character is depicted in scenes of explicit sexuality which may be abhorrent to the actress. When she insists, "this character simply wouldn't do such a thing in this situation", she means *she* wouldn't, and the subversion of her own value system is so powerful she cannot distinguish between her attitudes and those of her character. Or, even if she can draw the distinction, her temperament cannot accept the experience of that immorality in what is, after all, her own personal frame. This has all the earmarks of a moral dilemma and since actors, like anyone else, have a code of morals (implicit or professed), it is common for contradictions of this sort to arise.

This is related to another aspect of morality that powerfully affects the way in which actors perform their duties. Given the role of, say, Claudius in *Hamlet*, they tacitly judge the character as being wicked and villainous. He is, after all, the usurper of Hamlet's father's throne, and the man who has "popp'd in between th'election and [his] hopes". He is the perpetrator of incest. He is the political schemer who tries to have his stepson poisoned by Laertes. And so he can be seen to be utterly villainous and wicked. But he is also the efficient monarch of the realm; the man who appears to have won Gertrude's real love and allegiance; the man who, initially, tries to reach an entente with the irascible young prince to enable them both to get on with their respective business. In other words, if the actor did not judge him to be unalterably wicked and villainous, his portrayal might well (as Alec Clunes's did in Peter Brook's production in 1955) avoid the melodramatic traps and banal choices which so frequently accrue. If the actor did not judge him according to his own code of morality, but let us say, according to Claudius's, a very different kind of interpretation would emerge.

And it is worth noting that so-called villainous or wicked characters in *real life* are not prepared to acknowledge their lack of morality. On the contrary, they devise elaborate rationalizations for their behaviour and when indicted can mount impressive defences for all their actions. Your view of a liar, a cheat or a scoundrel would rarely if ever be conceded by the person so stigmatized. More often, they rebut such accusations with indictments of their own, and suddenly you find yourself having to defend your own "virtues" in the light of another's condemnation. And then the ambiguities and contradictions described at the start of this chapter, are remorselessly put into play, and nagging, age-old questions like, what is true, and whose version of the truth can we accept, begin to proliferate.

The actor's act of judgment is almost always unconscious. It is based on prior assumptions, most of which have never been tested or even thought out. As an exercise, one could take an absolutely out-and-out villain such as Iago and construct a reasonable defence for his actions which might exonerate him from the guilty verdict generations of actors have passed upon him.*

What are his own two main defences for his destruction of Othello? (a) That he has been passed over for promotion in favour of Cassio (". . . 'tis the curse of service : / Preferment goes by letter and affection, / Not by the old gradation, where each second / Stood heir to the first"), and (b) that he believes Othello has seduced his wife Emilia ("I hate the Moor, / And it is thought abroad that 'twixt my sheets / 'Has done my office. I know not if't be true; / Yet I, for mere suspicion in that kind, / Will do as if for surety"). The first is patently true, and the second, pretty implausible – nevertheless, this is what he says he believes. Both of these "beliefs" are founded on notions of fair-play. A hard-working and trusted sub-

---

* See *"An Othello* Casebook", p. 163, for amplification of Iago's motives.

ordinate should get the deserts due him. He should not be passed over or, if he is going to be superseded by another officer, the reasons for this decision ought to be clearly stated. In terms of morality, if one thinks of Iago not as a congenital blackguard but an arch Puritan, one can begin to make sense of his attitudes – not only to Othello's supposed seduction of Emilia but also to his marriage to a white woman. The Puritan ethic, strictly applied, would be appalled by the act of miscegenation committed by Othello. Not only is it an act of disrespect, it is abominably anti-Christian – for doesn't the bible teach that kind should mate with kind? To an Iago conceived in these terms, Othello is more than a loathed superior officer, he is a genetic traitor as well as a traitor to the faith into which he has (obviously) been accepted despite his heathen background. And he is a perpetrator of the kind of licentiousness which must be anathema to the puritan mind. Given an influence as nefarious as Othello's (and the position of authority he holds), almost any manœuvre that can unseat him must be attempted. And when his plot is revealed, and Othello asks

> "Will you, I pray, demand of that demi-devil
> Why he hath thus ensnar'd my soul and body?"

it becomes the most natural thing in the world for Iago to reply:

> "Demand me nothing. What you know, you know.
> From this time forth I will never speak word."

For if the well-spring of his action has been fanatical zeal to a religious conviction rather than the innate deviltry to which it is usually attributed, it makes sense not even to begin to explain to heathens the depth of one's passionate belief. (Significantly, Lodovico's reply to Iago's ultimatum, almost suggesting the reason for his refusal to speak might be conscientious, is: "What! Not to pray?")

All of this is pure hypothesis – not definitive interpretation. But in acting, all one ever has is an hypothesis. There are no definitive interpretations of anything. And if one can construct a series of speculations based on a sympathetic rather than an antipathetic view of what is usually depicted as an unsympathetic character, the actor has an opportunity to arrive at an original rather than a predictable result.

The bar to original results is so often an arbitrarily arrived at, personally honed, objectively untenable sense of reality, that the most beneficial edict the theatre could issue would be a thirty-year ban on the use of the words *real life* – until such time as all could agree to the same definition (which would be never) or up to that point where the majority of actors, writers and directors might grudgingly concede there is no such thing.

5 *Audience Reaction*

One talks continually about "audience reaction" as if an entire horde of spectators touched by the same stimuli, were simultaneously experiencing the same feelings to the same degree. This never happens. One person may be responding to a detail of costume or a nuance of movement to which every other spectator is oblivious. Some people will be experiencing the theatrical *données* in so subjective a way that only depth-analysis can interpret the reasons behind their feelings. While one-third of a house may be laughing, two-thirds may be squirming with the gaucheness of what they consider to be forced comedy. However, to the ears of the performers, this partial guttural wheeze is invariably counted as a laugh "from the house".

Audience reaction is, in fact, a misnomer. The most one can obtain from an audience is a generalized audible response which, because it makes like sounds, tends to suggest a uniformity of feeling. The one thing which almost never happens in an audience is "audience reaction" – that is, a collective emotional and intellectual response so uniform it is the same for every person in the aggregate. But the purpose of the theatre-event (and occasionally it is achieved) is to bind together the disparate perceptions of its audience into a genuinely shared insight. When this happens in a comedy, it is easily verifiable. We have all heard – at one time or another – the sound of an audience exploding with the same comedic insight. In a drama or a tragedy, the shared-response is also possible, but its outward manifestation is much less distinct. It takes the form of a certain quality of silence; a certain intensity of attention which, at times, almost creates a shared breathing among all the spectators. This potent silence, this palpable sharing of sensibility is, in one sense, the objective of all theatre. It dynamically unites an audience because it enables every one of them to cohere around the same esthetic object thereby perceiving it freshly. It is the much abused "moment of truth", and what makes it "truthful" is that the inner sense of the outward event is so unquestionably experienced that even after one has left the theatre, its residue remains.

But this is rare. What is much more common is a sea of gaping faces each (depending on their naïveté or sophistication) receiving a spray of narrative and characterization, trying strenuously or lackadaisically to put together the dramatic information writers, directors and actors are dispensing. The lowest form of audience attention is that mentally fugitive state where events on the stage are continually mixing with unrelated events in the audience's mind; commingling thoughts of the supper-to-come, the architecture of the house, the number of scenes still to be got through before the interval, the waste of money, the staleness of the chocolates, etc. etc. The median state of interest is when characters and action possess enough sustaining power simply to interest the audience in the passage of time; creating an unpressured sense of wanting to know what comes next. The highest state of audience attention is that moment (and it rarely lasts for more than a moment) when a varied number of people of all ages and walks of life, unexpectedly discover a sense of unbroken communion as a result of a perception which has simultaneously infiltrated their minds. In that sense, great theatre is always educational. It reminds us, often in a flash of recognition, of certain private truths which, paradoxically, only become manifest in a public situation. Assuming it ever needed any, this interlocking of private insight through public awareness is the theatre's supreme justification.

6 The Confidence Trick

The actor is continually in a confidence-crisis. He has doubts about the content of his choices, the quality of the text, the colour of his costumes, the indecipherable look on the faces of his fellow-actors. He needs reassurance as regularly as the aircraft needs fuel – and for the same reason, in order to take off and stay airborne.

Many of the questions he puts to his director during rehearsals are in order to cadge this confidence and many of the director's replies are expressly given in order to encourage it. In some cases, a director's words of praise are genuinely motivated and confidence is legitimately instilled. But in many more cases, the director – sensing the performer's hunger for reassurance – doles out approval simply to alleviate the actor's distress.

Strictly speaking, this constitutes false confidence in that the director is merely trying to eradicate a distressing symptom with a convenient and cheaply dispensed tonic. The actor, bucked by the director's approval, is relieved. His work becomes more relaxed; his nervousness abates.

But that is not the end of the matter for, eventually, there is an opening and a judgment and often the cause of that original anxiety returns in a new and more monstrous form, bringing in its wake artistic failure and public censure. In acting, there is no carpet thick enough to conceal the dust that actors would sweep beneath it. The acting-problem that is not tackled grows and festers, and ultimately destroys everything around it. False confidence given to allay genuine doubts, is like Auden's "banished mouse" that returns as an "enraged rhinoceros".

It is not true to say the relaxed and content actor automatically delivers the best results. The tension an actor feels when he is "lacking confidence" is often born of an instinctive insight into a real fault in his performance and an arbitrary injection of confidence can become deadly if it diverts the actor from grappling with an underlying problem of interpretation. Lack of confidence, in a genuine artistic temperament, is a signal that personal choices are incorrect and/or direction has been misleading. True confidence never has to be doled out by directors like prizes from a benevolent schoolmaster. It is the product of well integrated, thoroughly thought-out and tested rehearsal work, the result of excruciating artistic endeavour. A happy actor who has suppressed the niggle of what, if he ever acknowledged it, might grow into a major acting-problem, and who wallows instead in the undeserved praise of his colleagues, is living in a fool's paradise, a domicile far preferable to the rack of creative anguish – which is the habitat of the creative artist.

There is no such thing as a happy actor who is also esthetically conscious.

Confidence is the infusion of self-esteem produced in the actor when the correctness of his choices has been confirmed by "audience reaction" and/or parallel assurances from his fellow actors that their choices are compatible with his own.

Nobody can *give* confidence to another. Anyone who seeks it outside of his own acting resources has a greater problem than merely, lack of confidence.

7 Seven Types of Non-Actors

Acting, unlike bicycle-riding, is one of those things that someone may appear to be doing while not doing it at all. You can't "go through the motions" of riding a bicycle without turning the wheels, guiding the handle-bars, locomoting from one point to another. You are either riding or you aren't. Acting however, has certain identifiable external characteristics which can pass for acting and frequently do. By the same token, there are categories of "actors" who dutifully don their costumes, apply their make-up, deliver their lines and comport themselves before the public without, in fact, acting — that is, truthfully rendering feeling, clearly expressing intention, enjoining palpable contact with their fellow-players and existentially defining the material they have been employed to interpret. The non-actors are legion, and if one cared to, one could draw up innumerable categories. The following are seven characteristic types.

THE SKATER

The Skater, inured to the meaning of his role through mindless and mechanical repetitions (sometimes preoccupied with extra-theatrical problems) follows the graph set during rehearsals oblivious of the fact that his creativity has been supplanted by a life-like but intrinsically dead automaton. His non-performance, all surface without substance, can still be effective, and there are innumerable anecdotes of actors who apologize for having been mentally absent on a particular night only to be told they gave the performance of a lifetime. This comes about when the forms of the production are so well chosen, the narrative so taut, that all that is really required of the actor is his physical presence. The grooves of the production automatically guide him to his destination like a magnetized pin-ball machine in which the little steel pellet hits all the right flippers without the players having to do anything more than introduce it on to the magnetized playing-field. Or, it sometimes happens that the actor's technique is so accomplished, it requires no inner drive to make its points – as if surface-truth were all the truth necessary to ring the changes of the play. On other occasions, the actor's personal preoccupation – although alien to the dramatic material – emotionally parallels his character's inner life. The actor's subconscious unwittingly nourishes the dramatic events despite the fact there is no active commitment to them. But this is a rare coincidence. More often, this kind of performance denotes an actor on a mental sabbatical whose body, zombie-like, performs the play's motions according to previous instruction hoping against hope a reunion may soon be effected with the absent spirit.

THE SIMULATOR

The Simulator, powerfully (often unconsciously) influenced by the work of a celebrated performer, organizes his acting-mechanism in such a way as to simulate the actions of his hero. This sometimes involves inflexions, emphases and "tunes" derived from the admired model, but is most disastrous when he appropriates emotional responses alien to himself but characteristic of the idol; an appropriation based on the assumption that there is a more effective way of registering feeling than that which comes naturally to him –

a fallacy that ignores the fact that no two persons behave in exactly the same way, except on the stage where theatrical convention encourages a uniformity inspired by fashion rather than nature. The Simulator, in recent years, has recycled performances of cult-actors such as Laurence Olivier, Marlon Brando and James Dean. It is wrong to call these "imitations" for there is no intention at mimicry. It is just that the Simulator has been powerfully affected by the way in which his idol plies his craft and has come to believe that what is effective for one actor should be so for another. Simulators are usually deficient in personality – hence the temptation to appropriate alternative egos. Also, they tend to think of acting in terms of masking rather than revealing.

THE THERAPY-FREAK

The Therapy-Freak, driven by profound but unconscious desires to materialize obsessive fantasies, modulates his role so that he can identify it with his most rampaging desires – whether they apply or not. Hence, if he is paranoid, he will see Hamlet entirely in terms of the conspiracy hatched against him by Claudius, Rosencrantz and Guildenstern, and play every scene as if the Prince were being led into a snake-pit or towards a camouflaged booby-trap. If he is emotionally repressed, he will inflate every emotion to ear-splitting proportions and find opportunities (whether they present themselves or not) to tear a passion into so many tatters that his fellow players begin to fear for his sanity. For him the role is the secret therapy; the performance, the encounter-session; and although there is an element of therapeutic need in every actor, the Therapy-Freak is the extreme version of the type without artistic compensation. Although eager to be cast in a role which he can get his teeth into, he should, strictly speaking, be cast into a mental institution, a destination at which he often arrives to everyone's astonishment – except that of his distresser mother, wife and attendant-analyst who, had anyone asked them, would have been only too eager to reveal the extent of the poor boy's troubled psyche.

THE PRISONER

The Prisoner, convinced the director has misconceived his role but unable or unwilling to resist his impositions, goes through motions in which he does not for one moment believe. Straitjacketed by "production" which goes against the grain and therefore unable to assimilate it in mind or body, he walks about the stage like a man wearing placards exhibiting manners and characteristics from which he would prefer to dissociate himself. To his friends, he may simply appear to be "miscast" or "not quite up to scratch", but in fact, he is not performing at all – because he has never made the actor's commitment to his material which is the prerequisite of any performance. The Prisoner should have the courage to quit if the director does not muster the presence of mind to fire him. Failing either course, he has no alternative but to pretend a performance and serve out his time.

THE EGO-TRIPPER

The consciousness of the Ego-Tripper is so firmly rooted in the auditorium, there is no energy left with which to forge links with his fellow-players. His consciousness of self (not the same as self-consciousness) is so pervasive, he barely acknowledges the presence of other actors. He plays *off* rather than with them. If anyone has the misfortune to look him in the eyes, they would find two glazed marbles whose focal point is somewhere in the higher reaches of the upper-ego where the Tripper is watching a fascinating film-track of the performance he believes he is giving, blissfully ignorant of the fact that it is not a performance at all, but an optical illusion created by the presence of an auditorium full of spectators whose seats happen to be tilted in his direction. It would be wrong to say that the Ego-Tripper is devoid of contact, for it is only contact with others that is beyond him. As for himself and the idealized conception of himself which is his performance – that "contact" is impregnable.

THE SHOWMAN

The Showman is not so much an actor as a man who has developed a wide variety of disguises to suit any dramatic purpose. He has his way of being jealous (furling his brow, flaring his nostrils), suspicious (shifting his eyes from side to side), frightened (tensing his muscles, hunching his shoulders, catching his breath), carefree (arching an eyebrow, cocking his head), angry (narrowing his eyes, gnashing his teeth), evil (smacking his lips, hooding his eyes, eating grapes), astonished (darting his eyebrows, popping his eyeballs, dropping his jaw), etc. etc. If anyone came up to him and posed a question about an inner life or the need to experience what he was expressing, he would think they were round the bend – or, if not mad, then certainly "not of the profession". The Showman believes, like the troupers of old, that the great actor is the man who learns to transmit those signals most easily comprehensible to the audience. He is essentially a communicator of clichés, but so ingrained are these clichés, he cannot begin to see them as anything other than the tools of his trade, the elements of his craft. Although one tends to associate the Showman with the posturings and preposterousness of another day and age, he is very much with us today, and his brand of acting, drenched in tradition and still acclaimed by the mob, exists as a constant threat to the spirit of modernity.

THE TALKER

There is a kind of actor whose greatest talent is not so much in what he does, but in what he conceptualizes. As a performer, he is often bleak and indistinct – a man who always seems to be acting in poor light even when brilliantly illuminated. When he is brought to task for lacking fire or definition, he proceeds to explain in a torrent of brilliant language, what the "idea" of his performance was. Often, this intellectual breakdown is so breathtaking, directors walk away from him believing it is some oversight on their part that they did not see what has just been vividly described. But invariably, the same murkiness re-occurs and, gradually, one realizes that the Talker is the victim of some unfortunate transmission-failure which makes it impossible for him to translate his conceptions into actuality. Sensing this inadequacy, he compensates for it by overdeveloping his powers of analysis. If concepts could take living form, the Talker would be the greatest actor in the world. But, as it is, his histrionics exist only in the elaborate rationalizations he concocts to obscure the fact he has landed himself in the wrong profession. (NB: Intellectual directors, particularly those with avant-garde inclinations, are most often taken in by this type.)

8 The Actor–Director Two-Step

Before rehearsals ever begin, the director and the actor have taken up their positions. The actor knows what will be demanded of him. He also has an idea about the size of his own expectations. It is either something he can do standing on his head (a repetition of previous performances based on the belief that this character is his "type"), or something he may have to stretch for (a slightly more ambitious version of a performance he feels he can give although may never have done so before), or a genuine challenge (a role of unquestionable stature or complexity which requires more creative gifts than he has previously been shown to possess). The director has his own conceptions both of the role and the capability of the actor. If he has merely "cast to type", it is quite likely he thinks of the rehearsal process as being automatic. He knows what the actor can do and he has cast him in order for just that to be done. If he actually has a "conception of character" and a hunch that a particular actor may be able to realize that conception interestingly, he approaches the actor somewhat differently. He perceives a course which has to be run and he thinks of himself as a coach to the sprinter who, to run the course successfully, must overcome certain foreseeable hurdles; his job being (A) to make the actor aware of the hurdles and (B) to develop in him the levitation required to clear them. If the role is sinewy and complex and all the director knows with any real certainty is that immense difficulties lie ahead, he may appropriate the actor the way a foreman does an electric-drill brought into service because a hand-drill is insufficient for the job before him. The director hires the actor in order to harness the power necessary to see them both through the problems that lie ahead.

Although the actor and director have both chosen their positions beforehand, they rarely discuss them. They simply proceed on the basis of their pre-conceptions and "negotiate" accordingly.

It is not uncommon for the actor–director relationship to develop into a power-struggle. Usually this means that the actor's conception – either of his role or his capabilities – differs from that of the director, and the director is not prepared to accommodate the difference. It is expected in such cases that the actor should either give way or resign, but it rarely happens that way. What does happen is that both actor and director take refuge in "third parties": the script, a personal conception of art, an even more personal conception of "reality", speculations about what an audience will think, fantasies regarding career "image", in some instances, an amorphous sense of "correct behaviour" very much like a code of morality. Using these "third parties" as referees, they endeavour to bend the rules to suit their own prejudices. Underlying much of this aggravation, one often finds a steel-ribbed presumptuousness which seems to be peculiar to the Dramatic Art: each person's unshakeable conviction of his or her own infallibility based on "years of experience in the profession" or some other such shibboleth. Sometimes the director simply has the wrong end of the stick and no one understands this better than the actor who is being beaten over the head with it. Other times, the conflict is produced because the actor instinctively refuses the director's tacit invitation to broaden his scope, to take a short trip on a flimsy craft round an uncharted isle and, for the sake of making some astounding discoveries, risk drowning. This is more common than actors will admit. Their rationalizations in such disputes are so elaborate it is difficult for them to acknowledge that all they really crave is to be left "artistically" alone (i.e. allowed to repeat themselves). I would like to remain impartial in this hypothetical dispute, but it is hard to deny that one of the theatre's gut problems is the congenital conservatism of the actor: a tendency to cling to known quantities and redistribute easy effects rather than gather one's courage and leap into the dark. It is an understandable reluctance. The actor knows what is effective *for him*. He has used these effects many times and because they have worked, he continues to use them. Although he pays lip-service to "variety" and is ostensibly moving from one role to another, it is often an unconscious game of musical chairs – with very few chairs. The fact that each play has new requirements and appears to be different from the last obscures the fact that the actor's behaviour pattern is unchanged. I do not mean the *character's* behaviour pattern, but the *actor's*; the processes by which he arrives at his characterization. Unless the actor is deliberately derailed, his acting-instinct is to cart yet another performance down the line and into his theatrical tramshed. His natural tendency is to *apply acting* where demanded; the assumption being, there is no "effect" he cannot achieve by regulating his instrument accordingly.

Given this presumptuousness, the arrival of a director with a wide variety of new and unexpected demands can be very salutary. The director's starting-point is not the given expertise of the actor, but the demands of the character in relation to his personal conception of the play. Assuming he is the kind of director who makes such demands and holds such conceptions, the actor is suddenly confronted with a goal which, being beyond his limitations, he has never considered. If he is brave (and artistically speaking, it is very much a matter of courage), he unbuckles his imagination, moves it along a notch or two, and accepts the new demands. If he has a timid or retentive nature, he fights tooth and claw to be allowed to preserve the dubious treasure-trove of his known quantities.

Obviously, there is no way of legislating for the differences that arise between actors and directors in the innumerable situations in which they find themselves, but on the assumption that a director does conceive a goal beyond the ordinary capabilities of the actor, it behoves the actor to make for it. Unless he accustoms himself to stretching beyond his reach, he will (to turn the metaphor around) find himself reaching beneath his stretch; that is he will accustom himself to less and less effort as time goes on. As for the kinds of challenge I mean :

In a celebrated German company several years ago, there was a leading actor with a strong proclivity for comedy. When he heard I was coming to direct *The Taming of the Shrew* he was delighted to be cast to play Petruchio, a role associated with endless comic possibilities. When he heard that I was intending to direct it as a kind of gothic tragedy eliminating all the comedy and turning it into a cruel, cold and implacable drama redolent of *The Duchess of Malfi*, he was stopped in his tracks. He had already envisaged a Petruchio which would be highly physical and overflowing with ingenious comic business. Now he was being asked to contemplate a daemonic relationship between Petruchio and Katherine in which the latter is methodically brainwashed and gradually dominated by a sly, conniving, almost psychopathic male chauvinist monster. The dilemma was clear. He was being asked to relinquish not only a different conception of character, but to abandon those tricks of skill and comedy-playing which would guarantee him the audience's certain approval, and to exchange all of this for an unconventional and untested interpretation which, even if it worked, would lose him the audience's sympathy as surely as it would gain it for Katherine. After a lot of internal tussling, the actor threw off his preconception like an old skin and gave himself entirely to the radical approach. He was able to convert his disappointment and surprise into a new initiative, whereas another actor might have proceeded from disappointment merely into resentment and negation.

Choices, very much less discernible than the one I have just described, arrive on the actor's doorstep daily; he can choose to work or to laze, to repeat or to create, to fight or to yield, to accept or to reject, and though most of those choices are conditioned by a combination of economic and ego considerations, the way they are acted upon determines the measure of the man and his potential growth as an artist.

It is politic for the director to persuade the actor without giving blunt directives, and there are many schools of thought as to how this should be done. One of these is the use of child-psychology. The director, using all the ingenuity traditional to his calling (?!), leads the actor to insights which have been carefully planted for his discovery. In that way, it is believed, the actor assimilates ideas more organically because he believes them to be his own discoveries. With a certain type of actor that method can be quite effective and it is certainly true that self-discovery is preferable to impositions from without. Another method is for the director to take the actor into his confidence and admit there is a serious problem for which he cannot find a solution. That puts into motion certain problem-solving machinery in the actor which, in normal circumstances, lies dormant. Often, this approach achieves a sensational result (arrived at by the actor) which is subsequently (in reviews, for example) automatically attributed to the director. Another way of obtaining a result is what might be called the Exasperation Approach. The director, after innumerable attempts to "get what he wants", throws up his hands and admits defeat. The implication is that the actor lacks the talent or the imagination to solve the artistic problem; the sub-text is that another actor can. This desperate measure sometimes creates a flow of inspiration the actor never thought himself capable of; ideas flow from a subterranean spring unearthed by the fear of dismissal or the shock-awareness of artistic inferiority, both of which are equally harrowing spectres.

But apart from these crude master–servant games which are incessantly played, there are other, more mature ways of collaborating with the actor. The best, as I've suggested elsewhere, is actively to try a variety of likely and unlikely solutions and, as a result of thorough experimentation, dislodge the problem. This approach is predicated on a reciprocal relationship between the actor and director; a sense of artistic equality which shuns any notion of superiors and inferiors, employers and employed. When the actor and director are locked into the same quandary, a sense of common purpose arises which inevitably encourages common solutions. It is up to the director to establish that alliance at the start and to maintain it throughout.

Often the existence of a problem is acknowledged by only one party. I can remember many situations in which an actor has come to me, his brow furrowed in anguish, asking me to help him solve a problem which, in my view, simply did not exist. It is ruinous to belittle a problem simply because it is not visible, and indulge in a kind of paternal back-patting ("Just go and have a cup of tea, and, you'll see, everything will turn out fine in time"). For, if an actor of talent *feels* a problem and the director cannot see it, it will eventually loom before him like a behemoth; because a genuinely felt problem never goes away, it increases in magnitude almost in direct ratio to the degree to which it is avoided by the director. Often, the problem is not couched articulately by the actor – which is why the director cannot comprehend it. But if rehearsal time is allotted to explore the source of the discontent, it often appears that there *is* a problem, and one so subtle, it has not yet become apparent to the director. The actor is the best guide to the chemistry of the performance, but the director is so busy organizing its dramatic effects, he frequently ignores the human ingredients out of which these effects are created. Where he may be insisting upon an acceleration of tempo or a pause, the actor is preoccupied with a tangle of inner complexities that prevents an acceleration or prohibits a pause. If there is a good internal reason why an actor feels he cannot produce a certain effect, the director should take the time to understand it. If he doesn't, if he simply ploughs over objections for the sake of some arbitrary master-plan, he is not only nullifying the nature of the collaboration, but sowing the seeds of later problems.

There are some directors who refuse to employ critical or analytical language in their work with actors. They feel, rightly or wrongly, that a critical analysis is not the best way to achieve results. They develop a shorthand which is every bit as effective as a long-winded intellectual commentary. "You're Humphrey Bogart here, just clocking Lauren Bacall's arrival", "Let's have a touch of the Jimmy Stewarts here", "This is where you beat up the eggs just before you throw the omelette into the pan", "Stay in third for as long as you can then throw yourself into overdrive", "Begin with the woodwinds then slowly bring in the brass section". All of these non-technical, ostensibly inexplicit comments contain for the director (and for the actor who shares the same frame of reference), a world of esthetic significance. The point is to know your actors well enough to realize when you can use shorthand and when it is necessary to be technically explanatory. What is fatal is talking to an actor on the assumption that he automatically shares your frame of reference – for instance, assuming that he has read Diderot or Aristotle; is thoroughly *au fait* with T. S. Eliot and "objective correlatives" – for actors talked to in this manner rarely reply, "I haven't a clue what you're talking about!" They usually nod sagely,

Stanislavsky as Vershinin in *The Three Sisters*
(*Mander and Mitchenson Theatre Collection*)

Scene from the original production of *The Seagull* at the
Moscow Arts Theatre, with Stanislavsky as Trigorin
(*Mander and Mitchenson Theatre Collection*)

Gertrude and the Ghost in a scene from *The Marowitz Hamlet* at the Open Space Theatre (*Photo Donald Cooper*)

Claudius, Guildenstern and Rosencrantz, with Hamlet in the
background, in *The Marowitz Hamlet*
(*Photo Donald Cooper*)

Gertrude, Hamlet and Ophelia in *The Marowitz Hamlet*
(*Photo Donald Cooper*)

appear to assimilate every nuance then turn around to their colleagues, register a look of utter bewilderment and walk off cursing
the jackass of a director who cannot talk in plain English. The actor
has his own language, his own "principles", his own value-system.
Unless the director learns them, there can never be true communication. The alternative is for the director to take the time to teach the
actor a whole new vernacular and, by so doing, assure himself that
both are talking the same language.

There are some actors who only produce the goods if they
experience approval. No matter how atrocious their performance
may be, it will not remedy itself unless criticism is prefaced with a
spray of compliments for what has already been accomplished.
There are other actors with strong masochistic streaks who wish to
hear only criticisms. They are happiest being lacerated by directors
who fiercely exhort them to pull their finger out, to change, to eliminate, to improve. There are some who resist every kind of emotional
intimidation – who can only be reached by the path of pure reason,
who respond only to the dulcet tones of rational analysis. There are
those who demand love, who blossom when they are embraced or
cuddled, who try all the harder when they feel themselves affirmed
as human beings. There are those who are thoroughly inaccessible;
whose arrogance is such that no criticism can penetrate their super-
ego. (Often these are the ones who listen most intently and appear
to agree with everything that is being said. Only the absence of any
change in their performance indicates the tenacity of their beliefs.)
There are those who can only grasp technical advice. They understand "slower" and "faster", "more" or "less" and they respond
efficiently to simple adverbs. It is a waste of time delving any deeper.
Every actor speaks his own language, responds to one tone of voice,
tunes out another. This, essentially, is what communication is all
about in the actor–director relationship and it is foolhardy to
believe that because people share the same language, they are able
to communicate with one another. The entire history of modern
times confirms the fallacy of that belief.

Finally (and tentatively), I would say a final word about the
emotional temperature of rehearsals.

The best productions I have assembled, the ones that have come
closest to satisfying my own desires, have invariably been conflict
laden. The worst have been remarkably free of conflict. It is as if

a production, in order to reach that sphere where art truly holds sway, has to undergo a series of tremendous convulsions; as if the only way it can be wrenched into being is through temper and turmoil; as if the only kind of performance worth its salt is one in which actors arrive at the first night with bruises on their psyche and blood on their hands. This may be romanticism and therefore, I warn the reader accordingly. But judging strictly from my own experience, I find there is a state of artistic health which comes about only as the aftermath of an agonizing seizure, and that there is a kind of resolution in the theatre which pervades only those products which have been racked by crises. Quite possibly, other directors with other experiences will be able to disprove this view and, I repeat, I am not putting forward a prescription but merely a personal observation. Believing this to be true, there have been occasions when some irrestistible perversity in my nature has caused me to manufacture a crisis in order to banish that atmosphere of uneventful tranquillity which was settling over my work. For me, the most terrifying of all warning-signals is silence; that kind of easy-going, measured silence that encourages cosy feelings and comfy banter around the tea-trolley. I am prepared to accept the possibility that tangible artistic achievement can flourish in such atmospheres, but it has not been my experience. When I reflect on what *has* been my experience, I draw the conclusion that an art which concerns itself with the manipulation of tensions and the conscious evocation of crisis in order to arouse the strongest possible feelings in a placid public, such an art must generate some of those elements in its process. Therefore, for me, conflict with actors and crisis in production is not a deplorable state of affairs, but one that suggests the right kind of chemical combustions are taking place.

9 The Rehearsal Process

FIRST PHASE

The first rehearsal is the push of the button that starts the mechanism a director has been assembling months, sometimes years in advance. It is obligatory, with actors in attendance, a designer at hand, a script on the table, for a start to be made. But what kind of start and towards what destination?

The "first reading", it is said, is as good a start as any. The common article, the play, held loosely or tightly (depending on individual tensions) is the shared object of the initiation rite. What is read, spoken or muttered during those first two hours is less important than the fact that they are got through. A start, of some sort, has been made. After that, work can begin.

But a first reading is not the only kind of opening ritual available for actors and, in many ways, it is the worst. For, being the traditional commencement of activities, it tends to instigate a mechanical repetition of theatrical process. The reading will lead to the discussion, to the blocking, to the memorization, to the run-through, to the dress-rehearsal, to the performance. Within that régime, one concedes, there are innumerable possibilities but, in a sense, there are even more if one resists the régime altogether. If one withholds from the actor the security he finds in familiar custom, if one prevents him from going through the motions he automatically associates with "work", it is possible to lead him to an entirely new threshold and from there to a very different level of work. As with audiences whose expectations are frustrated and who are then forced to make new adjustments from which they unexpectedly derive new insights, so the actor can sometimes stumble on to a completely new esthetic as a result of having his routine violently disrupted.

Obviously, there are no fixed rules for avoiding commencement; if there were, it would be a contradictory stratagem. Each project suggests the ways in which actors should start their work. When, for instance, I have been involved with the rehearsal of collage-adaptations of Shakespeare, my own priorities were clear. It was necessary for me to introduce actors to a different style of playing than that to which they were accustomed; one had, deliberately, to distance them from Aristotelian continuity (a beginning, a middle, an end); therefore a series of sound-and-movement improvisations, opposed to naturalistic sequence and progressive development, served my purposes. At these rehearsals, the first few hours were taken up with a variety of games and diversions which, on the face of it, appeared to have nothing to do with rehearsal at all. But embedded in these games and exercises, was the theatrical syntax out of which the production would eventually be constructed; the "feel" of discontinuity, the sense of putting together acting fragments without regard to consistency, the underlying implication that language was not the be-all and end-all of this particular theatrical project.

Another advantage to this kind of commencement is something that rarely happens in the early stages of rehearsal (and sometimes never happens at all); namely, an awareness of the group's collective identity and precisely how each individual actor contributes to it. Call it "togetherness" or "group-feeling" or any name you like, but the basic component in any rehearsal period is the cog that moves each spoke of the wheel; the hidden matrix from which every wave of energy emanates and returns. The sense of common purpose.

Although usually taken for granted, this sense does not always exist in companies, and very rarely exists in *ad hoc* companies. An assorted group of actors arrive at a first rehearsal with an incalculable degree of inner turmoil. Ego-crises, uncertainty, fear of inadequacy, fear of disapproval, fear of the unknown . . . the interior elements swirling beneath the surface are endless. Suddenly, all of these psychic strands must be pulled together in order to harness the collective energy out of which a production will be shaped. What is more, the source of this energy has to be tapped so that it will flow into the proper channel; towards the creation of the style the director has already chosen for his production. Of all the rehearsal tasks, this is the most harrowing. How to capture these squirming, multi-faceted demons and muster them into the service of art!

There are countless ways of trying. Here are some :

Warm-Up

The company divides into two parallel lines so that each actor is facing a partner. One line is designated as Group A; the other as Group B.

Group A is asked to begin making movements with only one part of the body (i.e. the neck, the pelvis, the chest, the right arm, etc.) encouraged to localize the muscles of that part of the body and prevent movement everywhere else. Group B duplicates these movements exactly as in a mirror image. Eventually, Group B initiates movements using other localized parts of the body and Group A follows. (The graduation of the exercise should be from the muscles of the face, to the neck, arms, chest, trunk, legs, eventually incorporating the entire body in ascents and descents, jumps, turns, etc.)

Group A is then asked to transform their face into a mask, a rigid, stylized expression which exaggerates a particular emotion or attitude. Group B is obliged to react to this mask with a mask of their own provoked by Group A's expression. Eventually a "dialogue of masks" ensues – each actor taking as his cue the mask projected by his partner. Eventually, sounds which correspond to the attitudes expressed in the masks are added and the two groups encouraged to extend their "dialogues" into full-scale movement. (The company should be exhorted, at all times, to use sounds and masks as *reactions* to what they are receiving from their partners so as to avoid the registration of arbitrary attitudes).

This exercise is the equivalent of conventional physical limbering. The same result is produced through theatrical games rather than an overt form of physical-training. This means that apart from just getting an actor's body lubricated, it also begins to limber his imagination. Pure physical training, by concentrating exclusively on the body, often encourages the mind to abstain itself or to wander aimlessly.

Changing Circle

The actors form a circle around the periphery of the room. They are then told that someone, somewhere will initiate a repeated sound-and-movement into the centre of the circle, and that as soon as this sound-and-movement is begun, it will start simultaneously, with each actor, at every point in the circle. No one should begin it. It should just begin. Once the circle has moved to the centre of the room, each actor having duplicated the instigating sound-and-movement, the group stops and waits. After a few seconds, a different sound-and-movement will be initiated from somewhere else in the circle and the entire group, now performing the new sound-and-movement, will return to the periphery of the circle. The exercise continues with different sounds-and-movements taking the group to and from the centre of the room with constantly changing sounds and movements. Eventually, the time-gaps between each choice are eliminated so that the circle is continuously contracting and expanding with no thinking-time whatsoever.

The first value of this exercise comes in those early moments when everyone, their antennae scanning the room, is straining to see from where the first sound-and-movement will originate. The second value comes at the end, when the group, hopefully tuned into each other's rhythms, makes split-second changes without consciously preparing them.

Comedy and Tragedy

The company stands in a circle around the room. Actor A comes into the centre and begins to develop a repeated sound-and-movement, the spirit of which is comic. Once he has sculpted his sound-and-movement to his own satisfaction (and can account for every part of it), he brings it to another person in the circle (Actor B) and, still performing it, proceeds to teach it to Actor B. When he is satisfied that Actor B has duplicated it in every particular, Actor A takes the place of Actor B and Actor B, now performing Actor A's original sound-and-movement, moves to the centre of the circle. Gradually, stage by stage, he begins to transform Actor A's comic sound-and-movement into a tragic sound-and-movement. (The crunch of the exercise is the delicate graduation of Actor A's invention into Actor B's reversal of it. It must not slide or snap into the tragic sound-and-movement, but move organically, in clearly discernible stages from one quality to the other.) Once Actor B is satisfied with the form of his tragic sound-and-move-ment, he brings it to Actor C and (as Actor A did previously) proceeds to teach Actor C *his* sound-and-movement until he has learned it exactly. When satisfied, Actor B takes Actor C's place, and Actor C proceeds to transform the tragic sound-and-movement into a new comic sound-and-movement; he then gives it to Actor D and so on and so forth.

One has to explore, early in this exercise, precisely what one means by "comic" and "tragic". A comic sound-and-movement is not one riddled with laughter – nor is a tragic sound-and-movement one drenched with tears and lamentation. Laughter is the result of comedy; just as tears are sometimes the result of tragedy. In the comic or tragic choice, it is useful for the actor to have a comic or tragic character in mind. He should be *performing* an attitude based on some dramatic source, rather than merely positing a generalized comic or tragic cliché. If the choice is dramatic and there is true involvement with the under-lying attitude, these stylized sounds-and-movements can be riveting. The company should be reminded that this is an exercise for actors and that within the framework of this exercise, a sound-and-movement is like a small fragment of dramatic material which, like any other piece of dramatic material, benefits from being played with concentration and conviction.

Towards the close of this exercise, each actor gives his sound-and-movement invention to two or three different actors; each then develops their comic or tragic transformation in their own way and gives their final choice to two or three new people. Eventually, the entire company is drawn into the exercise, each at a different stage of transformation from comic to tragic or vice versa.

The Shared Rhythm

The company is placed in a circle. One actor is designated to begin a repeated rhythm (not a melody) which contains a basic pulse – like the percussion section of an orchestra. Then each actor in turn is obliged to add a rhythm of his own, making sure that each new contribution in some way augments and enhances the rhythm already created. Actors should be encouraged to select their rhythms from different parts of their vocal range : to produce different textures and different tempi. Each rhythm must be, in some way, different from the rhythms already chosen, but all must *belong* to the group rhythm which must be carefully listened to, and which remains constant throughout.

Once everyone in the group is contributing his or her rhythm to the shared rhythm (and this group rhythm is being constantly repeated), the group, without overt consultation, decides to adopt one person's rhythmic pattern as the group's unanimous choice. (This will usually be the most compelling or dynamic rhythm created in the group.) As this decision is made, each actor gradually alters his own rhythm so that it falls into line with the chosen rhythm. (This may involve graduating from a quick, high-pitched rhythm to a slow, low-pitched rhythm. Whatever the distance between the actor's original sound and the one being generally adopted, the stringent condition is that he arrives at the new rhythm by stages, slowly altering his rhythmic pattern in order to achieve the change.)

Eventually, every member of the group is performing the same rhythmic pattern, the one decided upon, without group consultation, by the group. At this point, the group-leader (the originator of the chosen sound) gradually alters his rhythmic pattern and the group follows suit. The leader then takes the group on the move, instigating changes in both the sounds and the movements.

When each person is making his own rhythmic sound and the decision to select the unifying rhythm is begun, there will be confusions and differences of opinion. It will take several seconds, perhaps minutes, for the group will to assert itself on to one sound or another. It is during this jumbled period of uncertainty that the group's attention must be keenest. As one actor opts for a particular rhythm and realizes that the majority of the others have opted for another, he must gradually abandon his preference and, just as gradually, gravitate to the group's overriding choice.

Non-Vocalized Rhythms

This has the same basic pattern as the previous exercise except that all rhythms are non-vocalized; that is, the vocal cords are not engaged in the production of the sound (plosives, glottal-stops, hisses, puckers, clucks, sounds produced by the tongue on the upper or lower palate, the teeth, the cheeks, the throat, etc.). Eventually, a group rhythm is created, each person's non-vocalized rhythm helping to enrich the overall group-sound. The sound is then stopped. On a downbeat, it is begun again. Then the actors are asked to remember the sound they have just made.

Pairs of actors are then given cue-words (Night–Day; Black–White; Up–Down; In–Out; Life–Death, etc.) and instructed that as soon as they are tapped on the back, they must call out their word as loudly as possible ("Night!") and receive back their cue ("Day!") called out by their partner with equal volume. However, these cue-words will be asked for while the actors are performing the non-vocalized group rhythm just completed, and the object is to be able to call out the cue-word, when tapped, without interfering with the repeated rhythm which is their part of the group exercise. The director, meanwhile, moves behind the participants and taps actors at will; eventually tapping in very quick succession to apply the greatest pressure to give cues and to retain rhythms. Once this is accomplished, the exercise is repeated with corresponding movements added to the sounds and the same cue-words retained. (See Appendix p. 111.)

One virtue of throwing actors in at the deep end with exercises and games, refusing them the armour of their scripts and the cubby-holes of their private contemplation is that it actually makes people aware of who is in the room and what they are *actually* like – rather than what they appear to be like judged by the infinitesimal social-signals they tentatively emit. For when actors are encouraged to make their own sounds and express their own movement, the director and the other actors become aware of the peculiarities of all the individuals in the common project. You become aware, for instance, that one actor has a tendency towards repetitive, mechanical sounds and martinet movements; that he takes refuge in a sense of order. Or you discover, through sounds and movements, that a particular actress has a tendency towards wild, anarchic cries; towards the release of some kind of mad, corked-up energy; that, in the case of a third, her kinetic tendency is towards lyricism and languid movement; that for another, it is sharp and jagged – like someone using gestures as weapons to ward off threats. Whatever the nature of an actor's sound-and-movement, each person in the room, depending on their degree of self-perception, becomes aware of the psychic gist of their colleagues; not *what they are really like as people* (whoever learns this conclusively about anyone?), but what forms their inner energies take when released in a physical, spontaneous way.

The other virtue of this kind of letting-down-of-hair is that a first session, devoted to vocal and physical expression, actually releases the tensions which a conventional first reading tends to contain (although it eventually trickles out in social conventions, i.e. expository banter in the pub, or probing conversation-cum-gossip in the tea-breaks). After a few days' time, people in any common situation begin to know more about each other – but it is largely what they are permitted to know from carefully censored social discourse. Whereas in an exercise where the actor is not able to prepare his actions, where his natural impulses are tapped and released, something a little more basic gets revealed – and ultimately, it is this more basic knowledge of one another that the actors will be dealing with in the hammerlocks of rehearsal.

Before there can be anything else, there must be contact. Once that has been established, one can begin to explore the images which will recur in a more conclusive form in the work ahead. Before Joan Littlewood began rehearsals of *The Quare Fella*, she had her actors march up and down the roof of her theatre in Stratford-East, London, trying to make them aware of what prison regimentation felt like. Similarly, in rehearsals for *Measure for Measure*, where one was aiming primarily for a sense of moral discrimination, we began rehearsals by creating a trial situation at which all the characters were called on to give testimony, the subject of the hearing being the alleged violation of Isabella by Angelo. Of course, in the early stages of a rehearsal, the actors know very little about their characters; all they do know – or *think* they know – is what happens in the play: the storyline, the events which have been dramatized. A judicial inquiry, couched in the terms of the improvisation I have described, actually tests that knowledge. It confers upon actors in a clear, existential way, what *actually* happened in the play, and it gives them the first budding awareness of what they, as characters, feel about it. For after the trial, the testimonies are ferociously analysed and the actors' improvised choices criticized by the rest of the company. The "mistakes" made by the actors in this improvisation become the basis for the choices which are eventually incorporated into the production. Far from being "mistakes", they are the removal of misconceptions that actors bring to the play, and the only way to root them out (other than truth-drugs or interminable analytical discussion) is to play them out. Immediately, the director be-

comes aware of what is going on in an actor's head. He then makes
the actor aware of it. If it needs correction or modification, it is much
easier to alter because one has experienced at first-hand precisely
what the actor's conception is. This is of enormous benefit, and one
cannot stress how important it is to discover what is going on in an
actor's mind; what his attitudes are predicated upon. In rehearsals,
you get the impact of them all the time, but you aren't always aware
of their source. Something "feels wrong" and you try desperately
(sometimes furiously) to change it. But what you are attempting to
change is the *effect* of the actor's attitude while unaware of the
thought process that has brought it about. In exploratory rehearsals,
however, you become aware of that cause, and if you can manage to
change an actor's underlying conception, it is possible fundamentally to change his interpretation. Without reaching that underlying
conception, you are reduced to tinkering with minutiae and making
superficial modifications. It is the old truism about treating the
symptoms rather than the cause.

The first phase of rehearsals is the most essential. It is here that
steps are taken in what is either the right or wrong direction and it
is harrowing simply because the rightness or wrongness does not
reveal itself until the very last rehearsals in the final phase. The
play is, in a sense, a wad of dramatic vocabulary provided by the
author. The actor's job is to be able to construct theatrical sentences
out of this vocabulary, and to do this he has to develop a very special
kind of syntax. But what, in theatrical terms, is *syntax* and how does
one develop it?

In grammar, syntax is what makes possible the construction of
sentences; it is that arrangement or order which defines subjects,
predicates and other kinds of agreed relationships in the formulation
of language. In our terms, syntax is very much the same. It assembles
the subjects and predicates of the agreed action (i.e. the play) so that
comprehensible relationships can be created between them. In the
theatre, unlike grammar, there are innumerable ways of interpreting
the agreed action (the play) and so the making of syntax depends
very largely on how individual directors and actors see the material
before them. Using one kind of syntax, the dramatic vocabulary of a
play like *Hamlet* is about a young man who cannot make up his
mind and who eventually wreaks havoc in his kingdom because of a

personal inadequacy. Using another kind of syntax *Hamlet* is about
a young man who cannot bring himself to perform an action which
goes against his grain thereby posing moral questions on to accepted
precepts of honour. With yet another kind of syntax, *Hamlet* could
be about a man trapped in a politically corrupt society who tries,
unsuccessfully, to rationalize himself out of a power struggle. Or
about a young man from one generation who cannot subscribe to the
values of an older generation and, in questioning them, forces his
entire society to reappraise the rules by which they live. In other
words, the change of syntax, like a change in key-signature, can
radically alter the way a dramatic vocabulary is expressed; and these
changes can sometimes be as drastic as a piece of music performed
in a major or a minor key, with a twelve-tone scale or entirely by
electronic means.

To illustrate this further let us say, for example, that a company
is about to embark on a production of *Macbeth* which will be mainly
concerned with the black magical elements of the play rather than
its Christian or political implications. Let us say, for argument's sake,
that a director is intending to realize *Macbeth* entirely in terms of
diabolism, seeing Macbeth as a victim of devilish forces personified
by the witches, abetted by the dark influences at work in Lady
Macbeth and by the evil proclivities in Macbeth's own nature which
readily inclines him into manipulation by supernatural forces. Let
us say that, in this version, the murderous impulses in Macbeth are
only the nefarious symptoms of a spell cast upon him by the witches;
that he murders, not only for ambitious advancement, but because
he has been *willed* to murder by metaphysical forces beyond his
control; that what one is attempting to depict, in this particular
production, is a universe dominated by malign influences whose
fiendish actions determine all social and human consequences. (And
let us say, just as readily, that this is an arbitrary, even scaled-down
reading of the play which doesn't pretend to realize the full potentialities of Shakespeare's play – although what production of
Macbeth ever has?)

The syntax of such a production must concern itself with elements
of magic and superstition. It must try to clarify what we relatively
sophisticated twentieth-century people mean by "magic" and "superstition". It must attempt to translate seventeenth-century notions of
deviltry into terms which are comprehensible to a contemporary

audience and, more important, to a contemporary group of actors confronting such an audience.

We have plenty of material at hand. In the mid-Sixties and early Seventies, there was a revival of interest in the occult. We had phenomena such as Polanski's *Rosemary's Baby*, a spate of Hammer Films dealing with vampirism, reincarnation and supernatural personnae. We had Charles Manson and his Death Valley "family", the murder of Sharon Tate, the subsequent Manson trial which revealed the depth of the family's belief in their master's diabolical potency. We also have things closer to our own experience. Our own memories of family superstitions; of what superstitious grandfathers and grandmothers believed and bequeathed to their grandchildren. We have, perhaps, unaccountable incidents from our own lives or the lives of people we know in which unreal and inexplicable events took place. We have the archives of Sunday newspapers where more notorious supernatural events have been chronicled or discussed.

The welter of all these memories, reminiscences, beliefs, opinions, anecdotes, old wives' tales and inexplicable phenomena would be discussed by the members of the company before rehearsals ever began. Out of these discussions, improvisations of the more dramatizable events could be devised. Voodoo rites and supernatural practices recorded in books or known by persons who have actually performed them, could be "rehearsed" in order for actors to experience their nature. It is easy enough to dismiss black magic rituals as a "concept", quite another thing to recreate one under the guidance of someone who firmly believes in their potency. (During a South African production of this play, I visited the home of Creda Mutwe, the Medicine-Man of the Zulu tribe, and asked him to show me a spell which might be used in order to destroy the sanity of an enemy, a scene which figured in my own production of *Macbeth*. Through the intercession of a mutual friend the request was granted and I returned to my company with the elements of a "spell" which was to be incorporated into the production; words and gestures I could not possibly have invented myself. The actors, all of whom were South Africans, were genuinely distressed by what I showed them. They questioned the wisdom of incorporating a real spell in what, after all, was a theatrical production. They were frightened of the

spell. It intruded an element of "magic" that was real – and therefore, not easily assimilated in a project made up of conventional
theatrical elements. I managed to persuade them to accept the spell
and, in a modified form, it was integrated into the production. Every
time we approached it in rehearsal, there was a palpable sense of
dread on the part of the three actresses who played the witches.
Eventually, it was, through constant repetition, assimilated and became "part" of a production. Months afterwards, when the play
had already been performed in Johannesburg and went on a tour of
Bantustans where many of the Zulus saw *Macbeth* for the first time,
the effect of the moment was dramatically revivified. Zulu members
of the audience left the theatre when actresses began intoning the
words of the spell. Complaints and controversy grew up around the
scene. The fear of the Zulus over its inclusion renewed the fears of
other members of the company. One part of that production of
Macbeth remained dangerous throughout its run.)

Putting to one side the ethics of the question, my justification for
using such a spell in such a production was that a small flavour of
true magic insinuated itself into a work founded on supernatural
assumptions. One tries, by conventionally dramatic means, to create
just such a sense of danger in many productions, usually without
success – as the theatre has learned to assimilate all shocks – from
sexuality to profanity, from simulated violence to audience-assault –
and yet here, because the vestiges of a taboo still existed and were
shared both by actors and audience, it was possible for a production
to appropriate a tiny fragment of actuality without automatically
rendering it harmless through art (the ubiquitous occupational
hazard in theatre).

Since one of the main factors of a production such as the *Macbeth*
we have postulated is the domination of one person by another (or
a group of others), improvisations which test such domination could
be devised (i.e. wife with besotted husband persuades him to insti-
tutionalize ageing mother in whom she sees a threat to her marital
authority). In such a scene, it is true, there is nothing inherently
"supernatural". It is a matter of whose arguments will prevail, the
husband's or the wife's – but in acting out such a conflict, one could
discover to what extent minds are changed, not by argument but by
sheer will-power, and as will-power is an ingredient in *Macbeth*
(exhortation of the spirit world, "Come you spirits / That tend on

mortal thoughts / Unsex me here", etc. etc.), an ingredient from such an improvisation can trickle into a performance and strengthen its fibre.

And this, in a fundamental sense, is what the development of syntax is for: to experience, in a primal way, the emotions and ideas which will utimately colour the final product. It is only by experiencing the full flood of such feelings that one can begin to filter them into a performance. Usually, there is a presumption on the part of the actors and actresses that they already know these things, and therefore do not need to indulge in improvisation. This is unquestionably true. The underlying passions of any roles are "known" by the performers in that there is an intellectual understanding of what they are like. The point of the exercises and improvs is to translate that "intellectual understanding" into a palpable experience, on the assumption that a performance is made up of ingredients drawn from "palpable experience" in order to be melted down and recycled into the ultimate experience: the experience-of-the-performance. The greatest threat to any actor is the presumption that knowledge can be *automatically* transposed into experience. There is nothing "automatic" about it. There is no substitute for "having the experience" – either in rehearsals or in real life – for what is then transferred is living matter (psychic energy) as opposed to mental equivalents based on hypothesis or empathy, both of which lack the cutting edge of actual experience. The rehearsal hall is a place where actors undergo experiences, and the best rehearsals are those where the strongest experiences are provoked in the actors so that the living material of their roles is being existentially researched. Conversely, the worst rehearsals are those where experience is taken for granted, and actors merely absorb the lines and moves of a play on the assumption that the experience exists – potentially – in the script, and their job is simply to turn a key and unlock it. The great fallacy here is the assumption that the *writer's* experience, which has created the play, in some ways credits the actor with the same experience; whereas in fact, the event-of-the-play is determined by the living exponents with whom an audience will come into contact. It is only through the actor that any experience can be conveyed to an audience, and unless he has created his own experience in rehearsal, there is, literally, nothing to be conveyed – except the empty shell of the writer's experience: a second-hand experience.

That is why the most futile activity in the theatre is the writer's obsessive desire to cling to his "baby", the script, and see it delivered to the light of day exactly as he envisaged it. To do that, he would have to speak every line and be every character. As soon as he relinquishes his "baby" to a company of actors, he authorizes a large number of foster-parents to present his child to the world as they see him. The great virtue of such an act of adoption is that often *they* can see the child with more clarity and more objectivity than his progenitor. The extra dividend that performance endows upon any script is the collective imagination of the artists who perform it. The depth or shallowness of that performance ultimately determines the value of any play and, although good plays have been ruined by bad performances, bad performances have been salvaged by good revivals, and no matter how one slices this squiggly wadge of theoretical blancmange, the inescapable fact is the act of performance, be it good or bad, is the only way for the work to be known. One must destroy the notion that there is some magical track by which a writer's work can arrive, pure and unsullied by the hands and intellects of its interpreters, at the final terminus. There is no such track – except the fleet magical-monorail of the writer's imagination where splendid superchiefs run beautifully, and always on time, but on a circular track in the head of one man.

To return to the starting-point, the actor in conjuction with the director must develop the syntax appropriate to the play's end result. My example has been with Shakespeare, but the principle applies to every play – modern or classic.

Look Back in Anger by John Osborne:
SYNTAX: Class-attitudes in England – particularly those obtaining in the mid-Fifties.

SUGGESTED IMPROVS: Working-class young man with good education but no social status has reunion with old school-friend who has become immensely successful and now moves in much higher social circles. Successful friend invites working-class young man to his Club in order to relive old times. (*Friend's Action*: to flaunt his newly acquired success before friend who during school-days had always assumed unjustified air-of-superiority.) Working-class young man accepts invitation because one part of him is genuinely impressed by wealthy friend's social accomplishment; at the same time he resents his exclusion from it. (*Working-class Young Man's Action*: to belittle what is being vaunted as social achievement; to undermine wealthy friend's estimation of his own success.)

IMPROV: Working-class young man with good education agrees to supper-party at home of middle-class girl friend arranged by girl's well-bred family. (*Family's Action*: to make working-class young man feel as uncomfortable as possible as means of disenchanting daughter and making her see the error of her ways. *Working-class Young Man's Action*: to mock life-style of parents and values they hold dear. *Girl's Action*: to try to effect an entente between two irreconcilable forces.)

IMPROV: Working-class young man in a court-of-law, offence being insulting behaviour to the police, i.e. using obscene language in a public place motivated by drunkenness and uncontrolled release of class-prejudice. Persons putting questions to young man (the other members of the cast) are members of Tribunal; their object to probe as deeply as possible the defendant's attitude to established authority. (Each member of the Tribunal can choose his or her own attitude to the defendant, i.e. anti-pathetic, sympathetic, indifferent, mocking, etc. etc., so long as there are enough members who support the Establishment view.)

Hedda Gabler by Henrik Ibsen :
SYNTAX: Power Drives between matched and ill-matched people. Differing social attitudes to scandal and propriety, romance and respectability.

IMPROV: Self-possessed woman tries to persuade infatuated man to leave his wife without offering any guarantees in return. Man is tempted to live up to woman's idealized conception of himself − even though he realizes it is not justified. (*Woman's Action*: to prove that she can control man's life. *Man's Action*: to conceal his weakness while, at the same time, convincing woman he is the man she thinks he is.)

Death of a Salesman by Arthur Miller :

SYNTAX: Illusions of success fostered by misconceived social goals. Disparities of consciousness between fathers and sons, one generation and another.

IMPROV: (1) Employee interviewed by Board of Directors for top-flight position. Totally sold on American ethic of free enterprise, prepared to submerge himself in "the company". Subscribes to values reflected in Board's questions. Gets the job.
(2) Same employee interviewed by Board for same position. Compelled by straitened circumstances to apply for job but despises American ethic. Makes supreme effort to be the sort of man directors are looking for; eventually, under pressure, true values assert themselves. Fails to get the job.

IMPROV: Proud father introducing son to close circle of friends as successful businessman whereas son is only a poorly salaried employee in large, anonymous corporation. Father inflates son's position to friends thereby elevating his own status; son tentatively qualifies father's descriptions to avoid being oversold. Father ignores all qualifications, continues to inflate son's status. Son, unable to bear distortions of his true state, ultimately rebels forcing father to recognize his position in life for what it is. (*Father's Action*: to impress friends. *Son's Actions*: (a) to remain true to himself (b) to compel father to recognize this truth.)

IMPROV: Father now standing as candidate for Republican Party; gives speech confirming Establishment ideals and explaining how necessary they are for the country's continued well-being. Son, standing for Opposition Party, delivers speech critical of Establishment position and criticizing the bogus values which prevail in country. Third candidate, for coalition party, tries to cleave to middle-of-the-road policy hoping to attract support from both factions. (Content of speeches to fasten on to topical issues of the day which exemplify right-wing and left-wing views, wholly unrelated to specific issues in play.)

SECOND PHASE

Once the actors have experienced the issues which are going to be taken up in the production, work on the script is begun. Invariably, this takes the form of some quick plotting of moves and attempts at memorization of lines. Of course, it is necessary for actors to learn where they are going to move and equally necessary for them to absorb the lines of their role, but very often this phase tends to obliterate the important findings of the First Phase. It is as if some invincible and primordial theatrical monster suddenly takes over. This is the Monster of Expediency; the Monster that continually reminds actors and directors of the need to get a certain amount of work done by, say, the end of the first week; considerably more by the second week, and almost everything that is going to constitute the elements of the performance by the third or fourth week. This is the Monster of Habit and Routine. The Monster that immerses creativity in technicalities and imposes an unanswerable imperative which is used effectively to curtail all discussion and banish all hesitations or doubts: we've got to get the show *on*!

It is during this Second Phase that actors have to be particularly conscious of the ideas they have already unearthed. If there is to be any real advance, the choices of the Second Phase must be conditioned by the thoughts and ideas stimulated in the First. Quite specifically, this means that instead of loosely plotting out the play so that it has a track on which to run, the performers and directors should test every impulse to move, every instinct to gesture, every tendency to rise so that what are blithely called the "moves" (but which are really the physical constituents of the play's underlying meaning) can grow organically out of the previously explored syntax.

Rather than *finding moves*, actors should be resisting the temptation of stock movements — until the necessity for a movement has been thoroughly justified in terms of the play's inner action. Often the quick imposition of "a plot" creates insoluble problems later on when actors have already become conditioned to a physical pattern which is found in the final stages to be contradictory or irrelevant. The price one then pays for "quick plotting" is laborious un-plotting, and the anguish of trying to discover, late in the day, what should have been arrived at more painstakingly at the beginning.

The physical and spatial relationships in a play are vital choices. They determine the effectiveness of almost everything else. If, for instance, a scene has been plotted on the move that requires a stationary position, no amount of interpretation-probing is going to yield any real solutions to problems. The fundamental problem, the wrong physical pattern, must first be recognized and altered if the more apparent problems of character and interpretation are to be ironed out. If, to give a second instance, a scene between a boy and a girl has been plotted at a distance of say, ten feet and the intrinsic requirement of the play is that they are side by side, no great clamour of lights and buzzers is going to signal the "mistake". It is not a "mistake" in the usual sense of the word because scenes can be played between two performers at any distance, or with one standing on his head and the other hanging from a chandelier. But if the intrinsic need of the scene *is* for them to be side by side, and that need is ignored, one small unit (perhaps six or eight minutes in a continuum of a hundred and thirty minutes) is blurred and that cannot help but diminish the effectiveness of everything from which it proceeds. If enough units are misconceived, the total result will be artistic failure; invariably attributed to conflicting sources : the playwright blames the director, the director blames the actors, the actor blames the director, the critics misplace blame everywhere and all becomes a muddle of (usually unspoken) recrimination, at which point refuge is taken in convenient homilies about the "difficulty" of art.

There is one director I know who frequently vacates the rehearsals during that trying period when actors are struggling with lines, on the preposterous assumption that actors prefer to go through those embarrassing trials in front of stage-management without the director present. God knows what he finds when he returns because he has absented himself during the most strategic period in the whole rehearsal process. It is precisely when actors are struggling with lines, when the tendency of most directors is to settle back and allow them to "get the thing right", that the director should be making the most vigorous intercessions. For what is being *learned* is not only lines but nuances of thought and subtleties of intention. The actor, working with script in hand or flailing about wildly to catch the thrown cue is, during this time, actually formulating the interpretation which, when lines and moves *are* learned, will become the crux of his performance. It is at just this time that a foot put wrong should be briskly withdrawn and a "wrong reading" positively rooted out, so that a minor misconception does not take hold and infect surrounding passages of the play. This is not a time for a director to assume a kind of English sense of politesse and allow the actor to "get on with his work" for it is precisely that work – the formulation of the character's thought and actions – which is *his*, the director's, work. Consternating as it may be for both actors and directors, this is the time for the play's central ideas to be pushed to the forefront and not shunted to one side because the cast is grappling with technical things. In rehearsal, a "technicality" is an external feature which contains all the fundamental elements of the living performance; it is, quite literally, Blake's "grain of sand" that contains a universe.

Once the scenes are playing (i.e. lines are more or less learned, moves more or less chosen), the tendency of rehearsals is to fix the pattern that has now begun to emerge. This is probably the most delicate stage of rehearsal for if the overwhelming desire to consolidate can be resisted, there is an opportunity for the second phase of creative work to be begun.

There is one conception of theatre in which a performance is seen as a series of carefully regulated fixed points. It is as if some directors believe there is a miraculous instrument which actually measures the emotional intensity of individual scenes and the length and breadth of characterization; an instrument so precise it can provide a series of exact, numerical readings which correspond to the exact degrees of dramatic energy required in any given scene.

Now it is true to say there is a desired level for most scenes and a certain size to which characters should be encouraged to grow during rehearsals. But given the human factor, it is impossible to fix a dead-level to these scenes or an exact height to the size of these characters. One knows soon enough when a scene goes "over the top" or doesn't come up to its full potential. One senses that a character lacks dimension or is too overblown. Clearly, dealing with human material means dealing with constant variables. The desire to fix those variables at certain levels is, on the whole, commendable, but the attempt to fix them exactly, is deplorable – and, what is more to the point, impossible. The intensity of feeling that an actor musters at any given performance is subject to an incalculable number of internal and external factors. For instance, his own mood on the night of performance; the mood of the house; the size of the house; the temperature of the house; the social make-up of the house; the psychological state of his fellow actors; the state of the world on that particular night; the morning mail; the atmosphere in the dressing-room; the personal biology, particularly in terms of being fed or being hungry, being alert or being dozy. The list is endless and can be augmented *ad infinitum.* Therefore, given the fact that one cannot regulate the exact degree that any performance will hit, all one can do is determine an upper and lower limit. Let us say, to illustrate the point, that an actor would be functioning at peak artistic efficiency if he were to hit a level of 3.4 in a given scene. It is then the director's job to make him aware of precisely what it feels like to be hitting 3.2 and 3.6. The best way to do this, the most practical way of leading him into the area of 3.4, is to allow him to experience for instance, the excesses of 8.6 and the insufficiencies of 1.3.

To illustrate this further (and to leave the muggy realm of mathematics), let us say that the scene we are dealing with is Act III Scene 1 of *Hamlet,* the so-called "Nunnery" scene in which Ophelia, on her father's instructions, encounters Hamlet, with Claudius concealed nearby to eavesdrop on the proceedings. Again, the requisites of this scene vary with different interpretations, but for our purposes, it will be the conventional or time-tested interpretation that we will be using.

According to this interpretation, Hamlet is feigning madness before Ophelia in order to convince Claudius of his unbalanced state – either indirectly, by Ophelia's report, or directly, for those who believe that Hamlet becomes aware he is being overheard by the King. The scene, from Hamlet's standpoint, shuttles between a series of unexpected outbursts and cool exchanges of an intimate nature. As for Ophelia, she is usually played as being frightened by Hamlet's sudden switches of attitude; hurt by his hostility and realizing that she has mistaken his earlier protestations. The scene ends with a rhetorical release of pity and horror ("O, what a noble mind is here o'erthrown") in which all the mixed feelings aroused in Ophelia by the ambivalent prince suddenly erupt.

The acting-problem in this scene, from Hamlet's standpoint, is to be able to hit his aggressive highs and then drop down to intimate lows without over-playing his hand. His Action could be: to be-fuddle Ophelia so that the correct report is given to the King, or, using the feigned madness only as a pretext, to terrify her because, subconsciously, he identifies Ophelia with Gertrude and all dissembling women, and this is a convenient means of unleashing his aggression. (Or twenty other intentions more elaborate than these.)

Let us say that for our particular production, we wish Hamlet to be able to reach an aggressive high which is just short of hysteria; very much closer to pent-up menace; a suggestion that, at any moment, something horrific might happen – although it never quite does; and that, at other moments, one wants him to be able to drop his madness (almost as if forgetting himself) and render lines like "I did love you once" as if he regretted having to abuse Ophelia in this uncharacteristic manner. A fluctuation between menacing hysteria, and calm, almost touching intimacy.

The actor has to discover how far he can go in venting his aggression and feigning his madness; how far he must return, in order to suggest a reasonable becalmed state.

EXERCISE 1:
The scene is to be played in the most bombastic manner possible, a kind of travesty of what is actually at stake, performed in a manner which suggests the worst excesses of nineteenth-century ham-acting. All attitudes are to be exaggerated; all emotions, pumped up beyond the point of credibility. All movements, extended into melodramatic gesture; all language rendered in an over-stated and overblown way. (N.B. The exaggerations however must use the real attitudes and emotions as their springboard. It is not a matter of simply guying the scene, but extending as far as is humanly possible, its actual dramatic ingredients.)

EXERCISE 2:
The scene is to be played as if it were in a drawing-room comedy written by someone like Noël Coward. An air of casualness and nonchalance is to prevail everywhere. All attitudes and expressions of emotions are to be underplayed to the point of invisibility; as if the greatest sin these characters could commit would be to "show their feelings". The physical behaviour and gesture

is likewise to be modernized, and scaled down to the new style of playing.

EXERCISE 3:
The scene is to be played as if Hamlet were a thoroughly rational human being and Ophelia a psychotic maniac. None of Ophelia's responses can be in any way *normal*. None of Hamlet's behaviour can be anything but normal.

EXERCISE 4:
The scene is to be played out with appropriate music as an Apache-dance, with Hamlet as the aggressive male dancer, and Ophelia his brutalized dancing-partner. During the dance, the lines are to be played out in accordance with their own intentions, but adjusted so as to fit with the music and the dance.

EXERCISE 5:
The scene is to be played entirely in sounds; the sounds must convey the gist of the sub-text. Hamlet takes his underlying attitudes which, in the scene, are cloaked by his "performance" and expresses them fully in sounds which convey their essence. Ophelia also gives vent to her feelings in an unbridled manner. In the final soliloquy ("O, what a noble mind is here o'er-thrown"), the sounds delineate the changing ideas and attitudes of the speech and, at the same time, serve as an outlet for the feelings accumulated by her in the previous encounter.

In Exercise 1, if it is successful, the actors learn precisely what is too much. In Exercise 2, if it is successful, the actors learn precisely what is too little. In Exercise 3, if it is successful, Hamlet experiences a little of what he is making Ophelia experience; Ophelia learns, at first-hand, the nature of the aggression being loosed upon her; also, what kind of inner turmoil it is that never gets released by Ophelia in the scene (indeed, in the *play*, until the Mad Scene). In Exercise 4 the sense of hostility in Hamlet and the sense of being victimized by Ophelia is played out in direct physical terms, and in a form that bears no apparent resemblance to Shakespeare although all the same energies are involved. In Exercise 5, the primitive feelings that animate both Hamlet and Ophelia but which are barely expressed in the scene, are encouraged to find their full outlet. All the twisted and savage energy that smoulders in the Prince (that emerges, for instance, in the Burial Scene where it is directed at Laertes) is tapped. All the repressed sexuality of the obedient daughter, highly disciplined by an officious father, is released; all the confusion and ambivalence of being courted by the heir-apparent while at the same time being denied freedom of self-expression, is experienced.

What is the good of this stretching above and below; these primitive sounds and unrelated situations? What is the point of playing around the material instead of making a bee-line for the problems at hand, in the form provided by the author? What is the point of wasting good rehearsal time?

All of these objections, in one form or another, have been raised against such exercises; often, without an opportunity to make explanations (sometimes, perversely, explanations have been deliberately withheld which, in an inexplicable way, increases the benefits derived from the work – assuming, of course, the actors do not stamp off in a fury).

What one tends to forget about the events of a play is that they are a synthesis of the past and the present. We are given a character to play who is, let us say, aged thirty-five. This same character was once aged sixteen; he was once twenty-one; not so long ago, he was thirty, but we are asked to portray him at thirty-five, taking for granted all his earlier development. But what a boy was at sixteen, a man at twenty-one, a mature person at thirty are vital determinants in what he is at thirty-five. One cannot have a series of different plays written about the character at different stages of his development, but one can make the effort imaginatively to research his past in order to comprehend what he is at present. In fact, in one way or another, all actors do this with every character they play – whether it's only a fleeting obligatory surmise about his "early days" or (as it used to be in the American theatre) a 2000-word essay on his family background, his school-days, his first-love, etc.

The same kind of thinking can be applied to a character's emotional and psychological behaviour in any given play. He is never *only* what he is depicted as being; he is many more things than he is depicted as being. A reserved and unemotional character, in certain situations and under certain stimuli, is a wild and tempestuous character. The reverse is equally true about a wild and tempestuous type. The contemplative Prince of Denmark whom we meet in the early scenes of the play contains the impetuous, some would say irrational, young man who struggles with Laertes at Ophelia's graveside. The philosophic and humane man who sits with the skull of Yorick and considers the progress of death through worms and dust into Imperious Caesar turned to clay is the same man who is well versed enough in duelling to take on Laertes, who impulsively runs through Polonius, organizes the murder of his old college-mates Rosencrantz and Guildenstern and ultimately kills Claudius. In short, any character contains the opposite characteristics from those that distinguish him as the character he is, and one way of defining his traits is to define, with equal clarity, the traits he lacks. And rather than consider this theoretically, one invests the characters with those traits in order to subtract them. The *experience* of subtracting them makes clearer the traits he possesses. But perhaps more important, in removing them, a little tinge of the qualities withdrawn is retained by the character – almost like a residue. We know that the brave man is sometimes a coward, a coward sometimes a hero; a villain sometimes virtuous, a virtuous man sometimes villainous. The components of character in a great play are never simple; never cut-and-dried, black or white. At different times, in different scenes, different qualities come to the fore – like one of those kaleidoscopes that sometimes show green, sometimes red. The more possibilities contained in the characterization, the more the actor has to choose from; and even if he doesn't consciously choose one colour or another, the existence of many pigments endows his performance with the constant potentiality of many different hues. As a great painter once pointed out, there is a component of black in the colour white; and white, under certain conditions of light, can be mistaken for black.

For examples of the kind of juxtapositions I am referring to:

- Play Juliet as a brazen whore trying flagrantly to pick up Romeo.
- Play King Lear as a mewling adolescent (a characterization incidentally, which you will find not all that far removed from the dotage of second childhood).
- Play Hedda Gabler as a spoiled child aged twelve who throws tantrums when she doesn't get her own way.

- Play Richard II vulgarly as a camp-queen lacking all regal refinement.
- Play Lady Macbeth as a menopausal, suburban housewife who simply can't get it together.
- Play Ophelia as a shameless nymphomaniac who "covers up" before Polonius and flagrantly uncovers when with Hamlet.
- Play Shylock as if he were Henry V.
- Play Henry V as if he were Iago.
- Play Othello as if he were Doll Tearsheet.
- Play Hamlet as if he were Tamburlaine.

Sometimes in rehearsals a moment just comes unstuck. It is a situation similar to a muscle-spasm. Something that should be fluid is stiff and cramped. When that happens with a muscle, one is advised to massage – not only the muscle, but all the area surrounding the muscle. By freeing the surrounding muscles and restoring circulation, the cramped area can sometimes be relieved. Some remedies are even more circuitous. There are some osteopaths who can relieve the ache in a calf by massaging the muscles in the neck. There are some pains in the legs which yield to treatment in the upper or lower spinal column, pains in the back which can be relieved by pressure on the heel. Whatever one may feel about osteopathy, it is generally acknowledged that the nervous-system is a complicated network of interconnecting parts and that often, the best way to get to the root of a muscular problem is to apply oneself to what appears to be an entirely unrelated part of the anatomy.

The analogy applies in acting. In order to solve a problem of a high-intensity moment in a particular scene, it is sometimes helpful to lighten or trivialize the scene. To impose an attitude which does not apply in order to, so to speak, get the muscles flexing all around it. In a problem scene I once had in a Swedish production of *Hamlet*, I asked the actor playing Claudius to perform his confessional speech ("O, my offence is rank, it smells to Heaven") in a blubbering, utterly self-pitying way – so much so that the words were drowned in tears. In returning to the scene, the actor became more conscious of the feeling that Claudius was trying to keep at bay whereas before, he was simply making a frontal attack at what he took to be the King's guilt. In scenes where the text is suppressing some powerful emotion, it is sometimes useful to open the flood-gates and encounter the feeling head-on. One then becomes aware of why floodgates are needed and of precisely what thickness they should be made. The actor playing Hamlet in the same production had a tendency to play the soliloquy "O, that this too too solid flesh would melt" as a demonstration of indignation rather than an expression of self-disgust. The words came not from a troubled centre inside the man, but off the top of his head like a proclamation to the audience. I put him into the foetal position and asked him to play the speech to his navel. This forced it to change direction but the instinct to project the feeling rather than to work it up was still there. I put him in a sack and asked him to play it so that only *he* could hear the words he was speaking. Lastly, I put the sack in a giant wardrobe-closet and had him play it again. Eventually, he was allowed to return to the stage and I exhorted him to remember the feeling of being closeted in the sack; his words reverberating in his ears alone. Gradually, one began to get a sense of Hamlet's inner life, painfully piecing together the memories of his father's death, his mother's hasty remarriage, the shame and confusion it nurtured in his mind. The feeling of private self-disgust was there, but the definition of the language was soft and fuzzy – too private to make quick sense to an audience at the pace at which it had to be delivered. As it gained in tempo, it lost its privacy and tended again to become proclamatory. One had to retard the tempo; return the words to the private world of Hamlet. Then, abandoning the sense of privacy, one began to play exclusively with the organization of the language. The actor played the speech reciting all the punctuation; retarding at every comma; pausing at every full-stop. After many repetitions when the form of the speech had become second nature, one abandoned the recitation of punctuation; returned to the sense of privacy but exhorted the actor to retain the verbal shape he had so carefully delineated. Eventually, after many hours, there was a balance struck between privacy of feeling and definition of public utterance, but always, throughout the run, the balance tipped towards too much privacy or too much proclamation. In the effort to maintain an equilibrium, the scene gained a certain hovering quality which haunted it. By emphasizing the difficulties of the soliloquy, by making the problem memorable to the actor, one had created a moment which would always be special to him, fraught with pitfalls, constantly in danger of going wrong. I'm sure he didn't thank me for that. On the other hand, it would never be glib; never be sailed through or mindlessly gabbled. The attention it had earned in rehearsal had given it a significance it would never lose. It was the problem-child that always demanded extra care. That itself brings a kind of acting dividend.

THIRD PHASE

Testing the Sub-Text

When rehearsals have reached the point where the text is being played fluently, the time is ripe for testing the sub-text. This is the point where actors have already become aware of the effects they tend to produce; they anticipate their "big moments"; they have begun to enjoy their dramatic outbursts or those touches of lyricism which, they can already foresee, will move, excite or endear them to the audience. That is, the engines of self-indulgence are roaring like mad and little by little, the actors begin to sever the umbilical cord between themselves and the director. Soon, or so the reasoning goes, they will be on that stage alone and it will be up to them to "deliver the goods". The zealously concerned director will be gone, reappearing if they are lucky, on five or six "special occasions" to make sure that they are not veering away too drastically from what he has set, but the onus of performance will be entirely on their shoulders.

The foretaste of this responsibility is a very salutary development for it begins to nurture in the actor that degree of self-reliance which he will need in order to sustain his run. The disadvantage of that burgeoning impulse is that, freed from the director's vigilant control, the actor can now pursue those appetizing moments that were vetoed or cut down in rehearsals. It is an opportunity for the actor to be wicked as "teacher" will shortly be out of the room.

That anticipation is, in fact, as childish as the image I have just used to describe it. Although actors always expect they will run wild, freed from the fetters of directorial control, the fact is the rehearsal period has already created an orbit beyond which it is very difficult to range, unless one is resolved to commit outright insubordination. The interpretation of the other actors, the physical patterns shared by the entire company, the ideas contained in the choice of design and costume – all of these factors restrict the actor to the path already agreed. Although there will be variation of degree in one scene or another, even this eventuality has been allowed for by the all-knowing director, and so, like it or not, the actor finds himself a prisoner in the production framework. In most cases, a willing captive, and in an open prison where there is still a very large measure of personal freedom – although very little freedom of choice; the choices having already been agreed beforehand.

It is curious that throughout the rehearsal process this ubiquitous tension between freedom and discipline is always at work. The director has been forced to curb the excesses of the actor; the actor has felt the need to counteract the more arbitrary decisions of the director; the playwright has probably been impelled to restrict the inventions of the director; the designer has tried to resist the whittling-down of his more ambitious ideas by the director and the stubborn preferences of the actors for colours and shapes never conceived in his artistic imagination. Throughout, there has been a necessary and inevitable striving for greater freedom and personal initiative, and a guiding acceptance of limits and diminutions, which, in microcosm, constitute the fundamental tension of all art: freedom constantly battling against form; order struggling to impose itself on chaos.

It is at this stage, where the facility to perform the play without stop engenders the desire to batten down all the hatches and settle for what one has, that the testing of the sub-text is most useful. It comes just at the moment when actors have psychologically abandoned search; the moment in fact, when they should be zealously reappraising what they have already found. The testing of the sub-text enables them to do just that.

Let us consider here some of the means available to us in carrying out these tests.

THE ROPE TRICK

A rope, about ten feet long, is tied to the waists of two actors, let us say one is male, the other female. They are then asked to play out their scene demonstrating on the rope the underlying tensions of the material. If a character feels that, at any given moment, he is asserting his will on the other character, he plays out the assertion-of-that-will on the rope; perhaps by pulling his partner wherever he wants her to be; or lassoing her and wrapping the rope round her; perhaps by jerk-ing the rope forcefully. The girl, for her part, may agree that at those moments she is being dominated by her male partner and she may yield to his manipulations. At other moments, she may feel that she becomes elusive or resistant – in which case she would play out her elusiveness and resistance on the rope. If, at another point, there is a moment of great tension between the boy and girl, the rope, held taut between them, should illustrate this tension. During the course of the exercise, the actors are released from their staging, but throughout are using the text as rehearsed. (NB : eventually, the handling of the rope becomes a challenge in itself. Of how many permutations is the rope capable? When might it be appropriate to skip with the rope, make a noose with the rope, play a tug-of-war with the rope, or, by making a loop in the rope, turn it into a keyhole, a mirror, a crown, a wimple, etc.?)

The rope trick tells a director, at a glance, what the actor believes his character's underlying attitude and emotion is supposed to be. If it is incorrect, it is glaringly evident. One doesn't have to cock one's ear and try to make out the insinuation behind the inflexion. It is clearly demonstrated in the way the rope is being handled. After the exercise, the questionable choices are discussed. Often, the revelation of the sub-text through this exercise is as great a revelation for the actor. "I never knew you felt that on that line!" "Do you really think he's being aggressive there?" "Why did you pull me towards you at that moment; I thought I was supposed to be rejected" and so on. The rope trick gives analytical discussion a new dimension in that it forces the actors not simply to analyse the words they are speaking, but the psychological impulses they have offered up as the reasons for those lines.

Back to Front

The actors are placed at the two extreme ends of the room – as far away from each other as possible. They are then asked to perform their scene. When an actor feels his character is being drawn towards the other, he moves, in whatever rhythm seems to be appropriate, towards his partner. When he feels the scene is repelling him from his partner, he moves away accordingly. When he feels his character being open with the other character, he moves towards his partner with open arms; when he feels he is concealing himself from the other character, he puts his arms around himself, turns inward and breaks contact. The physical variations will, of course, be determined by the graph of the scene, and how an actor moves (what he does with his body), will be determined by the actions of the sub-text. The main objective is to separate each character so that they are not "playing a scene together" and thereby test the internal motions of each.

Back to Back

A variation of the above is for the actors to be placed back to back, and to move away from each other (never turning to look around) according to the impulses of confrontation or withdrawal found in the scene.

In *Back to Front* or *Back to Back*, the actor is encouraged to express spatially the interior geography of a given scene. We all know (and admit) that innumerable things are going on inside ourselves while we are having a conversation. Most of these things, when they are emphatic enough, will colour the way we speak. The inferences of our internal attitude will be suggested or proclaimed in the way we use our words. In the exercise, one is asking the actor to play out kinetically and in space all these inner convulsions. Often, the exercise will range about wildly from one corner of the room to the other while the scene from which it is derived, is absolutely static. If carefully tested, and the findings returned to the original material, the static scene will develop a degree of inner activity it might have been difficult to achieve otherwise.

Facsimiles

Stage 1 : The actors are asked to create sounds which are suggestive of their sub-textual feelings. The sounds must be played out in the rhythm of their lines – so that at any given point, their playing-partner can piece out what is being said and recognize his cue: the prompter, able to follow the lines-cum-sounds in the script. In Stage 1, the sounds, chosen to correspond to the attitudes being expressed, will strongly resemble the actual "sound" the text makes when it is being played in words; the "music" of the original text with all its prepared inflections and emphases, will be comprehensible to anyone familiar with what actors have already rehearsed.

Stage 2 : After the actors have accustomed themselves to choosing sounds that more or less Mickey Mouse their spoken text, they are asked to create deeper and more original sounds which convey the gist of the sub-text and no longer correspond to the rhythm of their spoken text. Superficial or obvious sounds are no longer acceptable. Now, the sounds must be redolent of the innermost cravings and impulses of the characters and their actions. If, for instance, a speech of thirty lines

Scenes from *A Macbeth*
directed by Charles
Marowitz at the Open
Space Theatre
(*Photos Donald Cooper*)

Marowitz's production of *The Shrew* (*Photo Donald Cooper*)

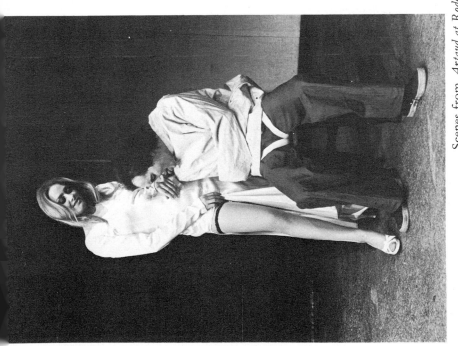

Scenes from *Artaud at Rodez* at the Open Space Theatre
(Photos Donald Cooper)

Artaud at Rodez at the Open Space Theatre
(*Photos Donald Cooper*)

has two predominant emotions, the actor, encapsulating all the verbal qualifications in his text, simply makes two sounds that organically convey what is basic to that speech. In moments where no words are spoken but profound feelings exist, the actor, again using sound, must express the texture of those pauses. If the sub-text is present, it should not be necessary for actors to "invent" sound, and the object of the exercise is not simply to see who can emit the most interesting noises. The sounds, if all has been properly prepared, already exist in the emotional sub-structure of the play; the actor merely voices the sound which expresses what he has always been playing beneath his text. If an actor cannot find the right sound, it may mean that the technique of the exercise is too alien to him; or that he is too armoured in conventional acting to function in such an unorthodox way. But in most cases, it will mean the sub-text has not been clearly thought out in the actor's mind – for if the living material of the scene is there and capable of being played in the dialogue, it is also there to be converted into sound-facsimiles. Often this exercise acts as a kind of X-ray, revealing either the paucity of an actor's performance, or the abundance of riches swirling beneath the spoken text.

Opera

The actors are asked to think of the play as if it were an opera and to sing their roles, inventing, on the spot, whatever melodies they think appropriate to their texts. Again, the point is not simply to "sing the lines" – but to imagine how the same dramatic moments might be conveyed within the context of the operatic form. Lyrical passages would be sung lyrically; comic passages would have an appropriate buffo musical style; "dramatic" passages would smack of the finer moments of Puccini or Verdi. The invention of melody is not a priority in this exercise; the point is not to make original music, but to find musical equivalents of what is being expressed in the dialogue. Also, since no one knows the tunes being created by their partners, their "music" must in some way (rhythmically, dynamically) correspond to the "music" being sung to them. Since all the dramatic requirements of theatre are also to be found in opera, there should be a musical equivalent for every moment of the play – even if one has to take liberties with musical styles and incorporate jazz or calypso, rock or blues.

Although this exercise also tests the sub-text by discovering a different form in which to express it, the main value is to the text. As soon as an actor thinks of his text as a libretto, he instinctively begins to phrase his words musically; that is, he imposes a form that modern and colloquial plays usually do not have. In finding a formal pattern for free-wheeling prose, he instinctively seeks out cadences and begins to think in terms of phrasing. The sense dictates the phrases; the music compels him to delineate them. During this exercise (which usually takes twice as long as the actual duration of any particular scene), one begins to hear words and phrases which have become muddied or glossed over in rehearsal. The end-result of *Opera* is to give actors a sense of the formal structure of the play's language in a way that can never be done at the rhythm of speech.

Ballet
The actors are asked to dance their text as if they were characters in a ballet. There is complete freedom of style allowing actors to select classical, modern, tap, jazz, flamenco, can-can – whatever is appropriate to his sub-textual needs. The rhythm of the dance forces the actor to measure out his text in accordance with the steps he invents. These "steps", rather than being interesting or remarkable in themselves, must correspond to the underlying dynamic of the scene. What is important is their accuracy in relation to the original script.

The initial difficulty in this exercise is that the actor tends to separate dance from speech. He delivers his lines while performing a dance but finds it difficult to make his lines correspond to the rhythm of his dance. This is an understandable difficulty since ballet is usually not accompanied by speech and actors rarely are also dancers. Therefore, one of the pressures of this exercise is for the text to be able to belong to the dance-movements which, theoretically, have been created to express the text. (It may be useful, at the start of this exercise, to acquaint actors with the dance options available to them : leaps, turns, time-steps, etc.)

The physical expression of sub-text is easy enough when the movement is free, but as soon as the actor is obliged to think in terms of dance he has to find existing forms which have affinities with what he is trying to express. The need to transfer verbal forms into dance-idioms makes him hyper-conscious of forms *per se*. Momentarily (or for the length of the exercise), he has to suspend thought in regard to his verbal delivery and try to come up with movement-patterns by the flow and content of his material. This engenders an awareness of form and gives him a useful vacation from the normal require-ments of his text. Often the value of this exercise is merely the mental release the actor achieves in regard to his text. When he returns, after having spontaneously explored the kinetic tendencies of what he has been playing, he comes to his written material freshly (albeit exhausted and in a hot sweat, thankful he is an actor and not a dancer).

As with so many of the exercises recorded herein, the "value" is not something to be methodically deduced and consciously invested in the performance, but a quality of freedom, a new vantage-point, or a momentary insight which will wend itself back to the work – in its own good time. If you tutor the actor on what he is supposed to get out of an exercise, you drastically reduce his chances of getting anything out of it. For the sake of a book like this, it is necessary to intellectualize their purport, but for practical purposes, it is better just to do them and keep discussion down to a minimum. Since the overriding aim of all of them is to create a spontaneous, improvisatory flow of feeling; it is lethal to announce in advance the results which are intended to accrue. Nothing destroys spontaneity more effectively than a spelled-out thesis.

The last point about stretching-games and exercises is that they can never prove their value immediately. That is, twenty-four hours after the improv, the actor would be hard put to indicate precisely how his performance has benefited from the work – for sometimes the benefit doesn't accrue for weeks or months. But during the course of a run, it has often happened that an actor finds a new kernel of an idea or an action appearing in his performance that he can trace back to an exercise performed six or seven months before in the rehearsal period. For the rehearsal exercises are like a computer bank which furnishes an insight or a detail when the unconscious pushes the button that requires it. And perhaps the reason the request is made in the first place is because there is a store of rehearsal experience to draw upon. The most dispiriting time for an actor is during the long run of a play when he feels he is simply repeating himself mechanically. A resourceful rehearsal period is a small insurance policy against this kind of sterility. The greater the riches of the rehearsal period, the longer the role can be organically sustained during the run. By the same token, a short, mindless *blitzkrieg* of a rehearsal period leaves nothing in its wake – except the daunting prospect of mindless, soulless reiteration. The actor who keeps "finding things" during a long run is finding that which was stored away during rehearsals. The actor who complains he is only "going through the motions" is indicting a rehearsal period which actually implanted the "motions" he is now laboriously "going through".

The First Phase has furnished the actor with his necessary raw materials. In the Second Phase, he refines them and begins to shape the product of his performance. Unfortunately, he is concerned with the most essential creative factors at the same time as he is preoccupied with the memorization of lines and movement. It is not a question of dividing his energies between "memorization" and "interpretation" but realizing that the one is inextricably bound up with the other. The *way* he learns *what* he learns determines the nature of what an audience will be asked to comprehend. There is no such thing in a rehearsal period as a time when creative probing is suspended and mechanical repetition is allowed to take over. Or, if there is, one is insinuating "mechanical repetition" as an artistic factor. It is hard to believe, but an actor can plant boredom and mindlessness into a performance just as he can build in excitement and stimulation. When he turns a blind eye to a nagging artistic question, or "settles for less" because he is too pressured or too lazy, or when he finds himself in a sticky passage frustrated by the writer or the director or his own inadequacy and "just can't be bothered" any longer, then he invites a moment of tedium or thoughtlessness to take up residence in his performance. Why then, four or five weeks later, should he be surprised to find the moment has settled in for good? Once the performance is on, the actor will be condemned to share his evenings with all those tedious uninvited guests. The prospect is truly daunting. It is bad enough for an audience to find a performance tiresome, but how much more wearying for the actor himself to be bored.

The Third Phase should build into the performance a consecutive series of irrestistible invitations *to play* – invitations so compelling and so energizing, the actor will be happy to accept night after night.

FINAL PHASE

In the last days before the performance, a second monster descends upon the theatre. With two hypnotic follow-spots for eyes, a cruel tangle of sound-tapes where his nose should be, a giant stopwatch for a mouth, this Mechanical Monster insists that all sign of interpretation now be banished and everything subordinated to his own carnivorous needs. With inflexible schedules and a great clatter of complicated equipment (aided and abetted by a storm-troop of painters, carpenters and electricians), he imposes an inescapable tyranny. The actors yield to him without hesitation. The director, after vain attempts at resistance, eventually admits defeat. The entire house from the smart-suited box-office manager to the lowliest ASM capitulates and soon nothing bars the path of his terrible advance.

The intimidation inspired by the technical demands of lighting, sound and décor is understandable. The technicians have been laying their plans as assiduously as any actor or director. They have remained in the background, been patient and quietly conscientious. Now that their moment has arrived, they grasp it with both hands. They have only a matter of days to assert their sense of priorities whereas the actors and director have had weeks. The performance of a play is all very well, but is it conceivable to have a "performance" without lights, without sounds, without every stitch of scenery firmly in its place and every thread of costume neatly sewn and finished off. Of course it is, but no one will convince them of that fact and besides, they too have undertaken "objectives", signed contracts, guaranteed deliveries. They too are "artists" and this is *their* moment.

All rehearsals are exercises in checks and balances; compromise is the *modus operandi* and conflict the inescapable condition. Throughout, one has been asking – tacitly or vocally – what is more important – my move or my acting-partner's line? My *idée-fixe* or the director's overall interpretation? My personal preference or "the way it looks from the front"? But strangely, this quest for even-handed justice tends to disappear in the wake of the Mechanical Monster. Everyone, even the director whom one would think most prone to object, accepts that a point has been reached where the performance must be frozen so that the Monster may wrap it up in transparent polythene and deliver it to a waiting public. Perhaps there is no reason for him not to. Quite possibly everything *is* ready for the screwing-down of the lid. In which case, lights, sounds and décor bring the final and fulfilling dimensions of the production; the external realizations of those earliest choices which have always anticipated their arrival. But frequently what happens once the play has reached dress-rehearsal is that unlooked-for problems suddenly emerge and, because these arrive at the last moment, there is a tendency to gloss them over for the sake of expedience.

The measure of a great director, in my view, can be taken at precisely that point when everyone's instinct is to push valiantly ahead to the last hill, and he refuses to let them go. This may take the form of re-opening questions of interpretation which everyone has assumed to be closed, or instituting drastic changes of direction at precisely that point where an actor's physical path has become irrevocably cemented. Whichever form it takes, it will produce consternation and anger. It will appear as if the director is deliberately trying to frustrate the actor at that most delicate moment – just before he is about to give his performance. And yet, if one assumes the director is not a sadist and that he genuinely makes last-minute discoveries which require last-minute alterations, the question of priorities (what is more important?) is perhaps more significant at this point than at any other. A director knows full well that last-minute changes, particularly to interpretation, can permanently unsettle an actor's performance, and that this in turn may drastically unhinge his own production. Therefore, he does not start on this course without great deliberation. On the other hand, what kind of director is it that has perception to realize there is a serious flaw in the fabric of a performance and lacks the courage to correct it if he can? The urgencies of time and the requisites of the production are both locked in a stranglehold. If the flaw is minor and the attention drawn to it creates a major agitation, the director is cutting his own throat. (And here one should say that directors are as prone to stage-fright as actors, and that whereas an actor, in the grip of performance-hysteria, may suddenly decide to play a humpbacked character without a hump or a cleanshaven character with a long, red beard, the director is just as likely to cut a vital ingredient of characterization or draw heavy attention to an insignificant detail only because his nervousness causes him to panic.) But if the fault *is* crucial; if, for instance, one suddenly realizes a fundamentally wrong choice in action or character, then to turn a blind eye because of the pressure of time is the height of irresponsibility. For the company's responsibility to the work does not suddenly fall into suspension while the designer and lighting-technician proceed with their own work. The lights, décor, sound and costumes must account to the *performance*, not impose an arbitrary rule. Here, the question of hierarchy must be emphatically driven home. The clothes are there to fit the actor – not the designer's sense of what the actor *ought* to be wearing; the lighting must fit the director's notion of what any actor requires in any given scene – not the lighting-designer's idea of what would produce a good effect. Every physical object, every tangible element, the choice of every colour and texture is there to serve the needs of the writer, as felt by the actor and perceived by the director. The production-team (the Mechanical Monster) is there to serve, not to command. This is perhaps most easily over-looked when the designer is a man of immense celebrity or the lighting-man a highly experienced old pro; the eminence of such men sometimes obscures the fact that they are subordinate to the artistic triumvirate of playwright–actor–director. To assert the true priorities, it is sometimes necessary to indulge in the kind of person-ality clashes that most outsiders usually attribute to the high-strung temperaments of theatre people. But, truth to tell, behind almost every tempestuous rehearsal row, there is a profound esthetic prin-ciple at stake. In more orderly companies, these principles are thrashed out before rehearsals ever begin. But in the commercial theatre (the scene of the more ear-splitting clashes), the collision of egos, the overlap of responsibilities and the confusions of jurisdic-tion are never properly arranged as almost every production is *ad hoc*. The great virtue of a permanent company or a pool of actors who frequently work with one another, is that – in time – a con-sciousness of degree gradually develops. Nobody ever quite says that the acting-ensemble and the director make up a single unit and the designers and technicians are there to support it, but through practice, an artistic chain of being begins to assert itself. Of course, it can all be broken by one ego-trip or the slip of a tongue, but it is a little more reliable than the catch-as-catch-can practice of the com-mercial theatre.

After the new revelations of the dress-rehearsals, it is useful to return to the rehearsal-room – without light, costume or décor – and examine the faults or inconsistencies thrown up by the runs. This return to basics might involve a return to the script, a return to the table, a "last" – as opposed to a "first" – reading. So long as the actors can be made to feel change is still possible, creative energies will still flow. It is only when the director intimates, by his manner and his schedule, that everything is wrapped up and what one wants now is solidification, that the actor exchanges his creative tools for the automation of performance.

In the final runs before the première, the director's role discernibly changes. All through rehearsal he has been, so to speak, in the thick of battle – on the stage or close to the stage, in the midst of his players. Now he sees the play from a new vantage-point almost as far removed as the audience will be – except that no matter where in the auditorium he takes his seat, he will never be able fully to distance himself from the play. Now his relationship with the actors is more studious; his view, more topographical. With notes in hand, confronting the company *en masse* rather than dealing with individual members, he returns to the concepts that were introduced at the outset. No longer grappling with isolated moments, he takes a general line in regard to scenes and when he refers to individual beats, he relies on the actor's intelligence to make corrections without his direct intercession. Although he is still "directing", he is no longer in tactile contact with the performance; he is now only in radio-control. His appeals are to the actor's consciousness of their performance, to their intellect, and to their powers of self-regulation.

This change of relationship, this stream-of-commentary which the actors begin to receive, is the first inkling they have of what has been created. The director's responses mingle with the actor's awareness of their own performance, and for the first time in the entire rehearsal process, both actor and director are discussing an entity that each can perceive quite distinctly.

This is also the stage where it is important for the director to adjust his vision. Unless he steps back to get a new perspective, the director will continue to look for the fulfilment of the choices he has made from day to day rather than seeing the result of those choices – the forest, no longer the trees. This is a time when he must relate all that he has been seeing in terms of performances to a quite new phenomenon – the production.

Although general notes can be quite stimulating and there is some value in a director delivering a critical analysis akin to what a reviewer might write, any note which does not contain a specific is almost not worth the time it takes to give. And by a "specific", I do not mean instructions like, Use the left hand and not the right, or Walk three paces instead of two, but a comment which contains a specific insight which is already part of the company's shared frame of reference; an insight into the substance of sub-text and actions which constitute the essences of the performance.

Now the inevitable preoccupation is with degree. This is the time to set levels, but in doing this, a director must remember that the volume of an actor's voice is not a question of decibels, but of intention. By modifying objectives or altering sub-text, the director can achieve meaningful level-changes, but to spend time trying to get A to act more forcefully or B to become subdued, is hopeless unless he tackles internals. "Louder" and "quieter" are convenient shorthand terms, but unless one deals with the acting-dynamics that produce theatrical size, the director will find himself trying to get actors to toe a line that only he can see. One run-through will be too much, another too little; the next, not sufficiently increased; the following just a bit over, etc., *ad infinitum.* The secret of giving effective notes (it is also the underlying secret of rehearsals) is to concentrate on causes rather than symptoms.

The giving of notes brings yet another dimension to the work, and one which can be beneficial if one is aware of it.

The actors all huddled around a director examining in minute detail the precise components of their mutual work creates a palpable sense of communion. The director's observations, and those of other members of the company, nourishes the collective ego of the company which takes an understandable delight in having its work minutely scrutinized. Harsh criticism in this context can become a potent demoralizing force. Light-hearted criticism which doesn't violate the fabric of togetherness, brings better results because an actor unconsciously appreciates the fact that changes are intended to improve the collective article, the presence of which is powerfully confirmed by this sense of communion. But what if the production is suddenly revealed to be full of flaws; what if the problems thrown up by the last runs are so enormous they threaten the validity of everyone's work – surprisingly, this can happen and a quite agreeable, even pleasant rehearsal experience can, without anyone quite knowing why, give birth to a thoroughly awesome monstrosity.

The obligation of the note-sessions is then to confront, without flinching, the grim realities that have been thrown up. Fierce

honesty in analysing a company's final product is not only salutary –
it is magical. The truth, spoken without rancour or bitterness, but in
a clear, unequivocal tone of voice can produce astonishing chemical
transformations. Virtues emerge which could never be born out of
the most laborious rehearsal sessions. The word of truth – spoken
to actors who wish to hear it for the sake of the common good, is
the most powerful force in the whole artistic process (assuming of
course, it connects with the actors' own misgivings and unspoken
doubts). Equally, the most ruinous sound a director can make is the
glossing-over of his own disappointment for the sake of fabricating
confidence for the imminent performance. If an actor who has been
tuned into the intricacies of sub-text for four or six weeks cannot
discern the sound of a director's mendacity, he is not much of an
actor. And if a director, having committed himself to weeks of
honest research, has the audacity to delude his collaborators at the
most crucial point of the proceedings, he is not much of a director.
No, whatever virtues may stem from false confidence, there is no
tonic to compare with even-handed truth-telling for the sake of the
common project. (This assumes, of course, that a director is able
to perceive the difference between good and bad – which often he
cannot. It also assumes a degree of selflessness on the part of the
director which, frequently, he does not possess. Lastly, it involves a
certain degree of courage, of being able to bear the "whips and
scorns" of resultant unpopularity, which many directors find an
insupportable consequence. It involves a whole slew of complex
human factors which differ from one situation to another, but I am
referring here, no matter how unrealistically, to ideal situations; in
the hope that such reference may cause them to arise.)

POST-PERFORMANCE

After a production has opened, yet another kind of tension sets in.
The director feels the need to protect his work from the vicissitudes
that performance bring, and the actors feel the need to try their
wings in a completely new ambiance dominated now by that greatest
monster of all, the public.

Although, as always, some kind of balance must be struck between
these conflicting impulses, it behoves the director to resist his anal-
retentive tendencies in regard to the production and, for the first

weeks at least, let the actors get on with it. Only they, in conjunction
with living audiences, can ultimately determine the rhythms and
size of what is required. In a sense, they exchange one director for
another – for a public is nothing if not a nightly tutor of how to win
or lose theatrical points.

The supreme danger, which has been lurking in the actor's bosom
from time immemorial, is the psychopathic desire to be loved and
approved of, and to satisfy this, some actors will go to any length.
And it is the satisfaction of these nefarious desires that produce the
excesses and spectacles of bad taste which make directors tear their
hair and writers contemplate the comforting cup of cyanide. (I recall
a sinister incident from my own career when, after having been away
from the West End production of Joe Orton's *Loot* for something
like eight weeks, I returned to find the lead actor playing with a
broadness and braggadocio which even on Blackpool Pier would
have seemed somewhat de trop. My exhortations to him were in
vain. "I'm getting all the laughs, aren't I?" was his unanswerable
defence, and it would have been perverse to try to explain that, to
achieve this end, he had reduced a subtle black comedy into a trouser-
dropping farce, and that the point was not simply "getting laughs"
but getting the *writer's* laughs in the style pre-determined by the
script and production. To this day, my hackles rise when I hear
actors talking about "getting laughs" – as if that virtue transcended
every other artistic goal – without realizing that, in a well-engineered
comic text, the easiest thing on God's earth is to "get laughs" and
the hardest, to make them come where intended and nowhere else.)

Nevertheless, and exceptions notwithstanding, it is the audience
who must dictate the refinements of the production – and if the
rehearsal process has built in the proper constituents, there is no
real danger to the run.

10 *Acting and Being*

Before we accept the equation that acting *is* what acting *does*, let us examine as carefully as we can precisely what it does.

The actor comes to a piece of material; a play. He experiences it as a whole, but not exactly because even as he is assimilating the entire play, he is entering into a special relationship with one part of it which is magically *his*. He comprehends the wider framework in which he will be operating but does so from the vantage-point of his role. He is already subjectifying one portion of the play while retaining comparative objectivity about the remainder.

As rehearsals begin, he digs deeper and deeper into that subjectivity. He becomes more and more immersed in his role. Theoretically, he does not lose sight of his surroundings, the objective work in which he has this subjective preoccupation, but in effect, he reduces his wider focus on the play in order to see his own contribution more clearly. During rehearsals, due to the presence of other

actors and a director who is obliged to maintain a balance between
all the parts (and therefore must remain as "objective" as possible),
the actor is constantly nudged out of his subjectivity and forced to
adjust himself to the subjectivities of others (his fellow-players) and
the objective demands of the director. Nevertheless, "working on
the role" means submerging himself in his own contemplations
even if, eventually, he surfaces to relate these "findings" to other
people. The submersion is a necessary first step.

What kind of submersion is this?

First of all, he imagines himself into his character's situation.
This is done more or less unconsciously. He perceives his character's
activities in a way that seems plausible to himself; the way *he* might
involve himself in those activities; the way *he* might feel in those
circumstances. The actor does not and cannot say: how would Joe
Doakes feel about this character, because he is obliged to work from
his own sensibility, instinctively relating the events in his character's
life to the way they might take place if *he* were that character. In
other words, he invests those parts of himself which are basic – his
mind, his imagination, his will, his reason – into another personage,
gradually transforming this "other personage" into himself. This
is the most mysterious fusion in the entire process; the submersion
of Self into Role, the delineation of Role by Self.

What next happens is a strictly mechanical process. The actor,
either by rote or during rehearsal, learns his lines through repetition.
This repetition becomes the main preoccupation for several weeks'
time. The actor continually repeats lines, moods, emotions, situations. Frequently, this repetition is interrupted by the director or
other actors, or the actor's own lack of efficiency in sustaining the
repetitions, but the imperative of rehearsals is continually to restore
the broken moments so that, before long, there is an unbroken series
of repetitions. The actor organizes his sensibility so that it does the
same thing over and over again, and he labours in order to make his
organism create these repetitions as effectively as possible; that is;
as involuntarily as possible. The actor endeavours to obscure the fact
that he is repeating himself. He works to persuade the audience that
he is doing what he is doing for the first time. So a cardinal requirement of this work is for it to appear to be *initiations* rather than
repetitions of behaviour. And to do this, paradoxically, he has to

concentrate not on starting anew each time, but on efficiently repeating himself.

Now we know that repetition is the key element in hypnosis. The
patient, put into a receptive state, is exposed to a recurring rhythm
or a regularly repeated visual image and eventually, hypnosis is
induced. The actor in effect, hypnotizes himself by repetitions of his
role. The fact that he is still conscious, still aware of everything going
on around him on the stage and in the auditorium, does not alter
the fact that his "performance" is the result of these hypnotic repetitions. When he is acting well (centred in the role), he is more
intensely *into* his repetitions than when he is acting badly (centred
in the auditorium). Should he wish to depart from his role, he
would have to disrupt the flow of his repetitions and this would be
difficult to do as *his* repetitions are coalesced with those of his other
actors and embedded in the paths marked out by the director as demanded by the text. So the actor is conjoined to repeat his repetitions
by the artistic régime which has been imposed upon him through
rehearsals. In order to "escape", he has to get past his other actors,
past the obstacles laid down by the director, and past the structure
of cause-and-effect implanted by the writer. Furthermore, he has to
be able to disrupt his own continuity; the self-hypnosis he has spent
weeks inducing in himself.

Artaud has talked about "a theatre that induces trance, as the
dances of the Dervishes induce trance". Like so many of his observations, it is an hyperbole at the root of which is a kernel of truth.
A constant wave of repetitions producing a mild form of self-
hypnosis is *like* the trance-state of the whirling Dervishes. The
difference is that the Dervish can *give himself* to the sensations he
produces through his movements and the actor instinctively holds
himself back. The Dervish spins for the sake of the trance; the actor
enters his trance for the sake of the spins. Nevertheless, there *is* a
loss of consciousness on the actor's part – which is what engenders
the alternative consciousness of the artistic creation (the role) and
it is this consciously extended alternative consciousness which conveys itself to the collective consciousness of the audience.

In the course of the actor's repetitions, he has been induced to
organize his inner thoughts so that they colour what he says and
does. The existence of the audience is like a potent magnetic-field
to the actor. It is there not only to hear his words and watch his

actions, but also to read his thoughts. The phenomenon of a group of people assembled together to examine a common object is that they develop a degree of group-consciousness, even if only for an instant, which is quite beyond the individual consciousness of any single spectator. The audience divines and interprets with a psychic gift that comes into being only when they assemble as an audience. They "tune in", they "react", they "twig to" – they bring a degree of perception which "sees through" not only what artists have organized for their perceptions, but also things they have not organized; things of which they themselves are unaware. An audience's radar sees more than it is shown, and what it does not see, it can sense; and what it does not sense, it can imagine. Confronted with such elaborate scanning-devices, the actor can conceal nothing – not his talent nor his inadequacy, not his enthusiasm nor his boredom, not his presence nor his absence.

When a performance succeeds, we talk about it "getting through" to the public, being on the audience's "wave-length", and these idiomatic expressions are significant. A performance that fails to "get through" or get on to the audience's "wave-length" is one in which the electrical waves generated by the actors are not being "received" by the audience. The physical performance is unquestionably there; it is visible and apparent, but its spiritual presence (i.e. communicated sub-text) is, to all intents and purposes, non-existent. Therefore what is (or is not) "getting through" is an invisible yet palpable communication which depends on actors infiltrating some intangible barrier created by the physical presence of the audience. This barrier is, of course, the audience's awareness of the play's artifice which a successful (sub-textually communicated) performance penetrates, thereby establishing contact with the tacit information being conveyed by the actor. Having "got through", having "tuned in" to the audience's "wave-length", a kind of dialogue is suddenly made possible, but the nature of this dialogue is itself tacit. The audience comprehends what the actors are *not* saying: what is being sub-textually implied; the actors begin to play, not to the physical presence of the audience seated before them, but to the consciousness of the receptivity to which their performance is "getting through". A tacit communication arises in a framework where an overt communication is taken for granted. It soon becomes clear that this overt communication is useless without the tacit one;

indeed, that it belies the other's existence; that the *apparent* attention of an assembled audience sitting quietly and listening, means nothing unless that attention has been directed to the information being tacitly conveyed.

Actor-audience contact can mean two people holding telephone receivers without any interconnecting cable. Or it can mean a one-way conversation on the false assumption that the other party is entirely engrossed. Or it can mean a nullification of communication in that one party is lying to the other and the other is not believing what he hears in any case. Or it can mean, the greatest deception of all, the belief that a dialogue is taking place simply because words are being exchanged between both parties.

An actor "addressing himself" to an audience means addressing himself to that part of the audience that comprehends his tacit intelligence, and this can be comprehended only by the existence of its counterpart in the actor; the discovery of his own tacit self which is capable of conveying the unspoken elements of which his audible and visible self is only the container.

I am not referring here to "implied behaviour" like mime, or gestures which indicate inner states, or stage-action which "carries forward the plot" and communicates narrative information to an audience, but to the quintessential centre inside the actor through which he establishes contact with an equivalent centre in the audience. On one level, this is thought-transference which is an essential part of all acting; on another, it is (what I hesitate to call) spiritual contact; that is, the establishment of communication with unseen forces which is so evident that neither the actor nor the public questions its presence.

Think for a moment with what difficulty a medium tries to establish contact with a spiritual force. There is the ritual of the séance, the darkened room, the holding of hands round the table, the group concentration, the exhortation to invisible presences to materialize or to give a sign. Whatever one's attitude to spiritualism may be, it is a matter of record that this ritual sometimes produces results — although the sceptic may deflate them and the scientist, rationalize them. The theatre works on a similar principle (social ritual, darkened room, communal presence, intense concentration, evocation of non-existent people and events) and when a performance can be said to "work", it is because it produces spiritual resonances which critics subsequently refer to using words such as "magnetism", "magic", "spell-binding" and "hypnotic".

Although spiritualism cannot serve as a metaphor for theatrical performance, the same kind of psychic energy is peculiar to both. (It is no accident that actors study Yoga, Transcendental Meditation and other "spiritual" disciplines, all of which have clear affinities to acting.) When people sense what we mean without any outward sign from us, we assume they are *psychic*. Actors are attempting to be psychic all the time. They are transmitting thoughts, experiencing desires, exerting wills, inducing states – and sending out all variety of emanations to an audience who, for their part, are psychically comprehending – or not – depending on the strength or weakness of the actor's signal. You notice that I do not say depending on the *audience's* sensitivity, or the *audience's* susceptibility to receive such messages, for I take that for granted. The arrival of the audience brings into existence one half of the psychic bargain. The other half, the actor's half, is where the real effort must be made. The audience are those people seated round the table holding hands; the actor is both the medium and the spirit through which it speaks. Bad vibrations notwithstanding, the state must be evoked by the actor. No sooner is it evoked than an audience can experience it. *Their* state-of-being is never in question; the actor's always is.

The most salient point about this psychic zone in which the actor manages to establish meaningful communication with the audience is that it cannot be entered at the last minute. The actor cannot suddenly "turn himself on" in order to "get through". It is in the labyrinths of the rehearsal period that the actor develops the interior vocabulary which will stand him in good stead at the performance – just as the audience has accumulated *its* interior cravings and potentialities before *it* enters the theatre. If the rehearsal period has amassed a wealth of sub-text on which the psyche can draw while the play is being performed, there is something to be communicated once contact is established. If the actor impudently assumes it will "be all right on the night", he is in the position of an injudicious host who invites several hundred people to a supper-party only to discover he has an empty larder. In a positive and irreversible sense, it can never be "right" on the "night" if it hasn't been *made* right during the rehearsal period. The divine bird of inspiration which may swoop down upon the performers on the première does so only if it is able to sniff out the tempting smell of provender. The rehearsal period is the time during which that provender is stored up. To assume anything else is to be a pathetic victim of the theatre's false mysticism: the notion that there is a gaggle of Muses (like unpartnered dance-hall girls) just hanging about waiting to touch the artist with genius.

The aim then is, by mental and psychic gestures, to generate spirit. But there is no such thing as spiritual evocation in and of itself. Just as there is no such thing as a "great performance" outside the context of a play. A narrative framework or a stylistic convention* is both the launching-pad and the recovery-vessel for all performances. If the narrative is implausible or the stylistic convention flawed, it is still possible to produce a "great performance" but only as an isolated act of skill. Henry Irving was able to transform an old blunderbuss like *The Bells* into a vehicle for himself, and throughout the history of the theatre, actors have had "vehicles" created merely to transport their personal goods. The actor of genius *can* transcend paltry material and produce "shows" of his greatness (as for instance, a great opera-singer in recital can demonstrate his or her musical skills) but the actor is integral to the play just as the singer is to the opera, and they can only realize themselves fully when the skill is being fed back to the material which stimulated it. The experience of great acting is always an experience in which an audience comprehends greatness through an understanding of things profounder than acting or production. You don't come away from a great night in the theatre preoccupied with an actor's stage-effects, but with the social, intellectual or spiritual repercussions those effects have produced in you. Great acting, like all great art, is a transcendental experience and not an invitation to mark scorecards. Indeed, if anyone ever desired proof positive of a mediocre experience, it would be the alacrity with which everyone proceeds to examine isolated performances.

Through the centuries, the actor has gradually altered his focal point. For the early actor, the centre was the auditorium and he emphatically directed his performance to that. Gradually, in the nineteenth and early twentieth century, he learned to draw himself in and turn his attention to his fellow players. In the mid-twentieth century, he was being exhorted to draw himself even further in and

* Happening-structure, multi-media, an improvised scenario, etc.

find some tremulous central point in his own nature. The excesses of the first period created the artificiality and bombast we associate with a crude and old-fashioned theatre; the excesses of the latter produced the unacceptable self-indulgence of the Method approach. It is tempting to think the truth lies somewhere in between, but it doesn't. The real focal point is neither on the stage nor in the auditorium, but in a state of consciousness which bridges the two areas. It is a plateau of sensibility in the audience which the actor reaches by climbing through himself and his material. There is no direct route, and sometimes the most circuitous paths lead him there. But unless the actor has some idea of the kind of plateau he is trying to discover, he will yo-yo between the tug of his psyche and the demands of his audience, hopelessly dividing himself trying to satisfy both. It may be no help at all to the actor to say it is a plateau where the audience and the actor's psychic energy coalesce, but that's as close a geographical location as I can provide.

11 The Actor's Prayer

O God of Thespis and Guardian of My Divine Spark,
Let me play tonight like the child I was
Before I converted my talent into a commodity
And sold my soul to Mammon.
O let me banish from my heart and mind
The overwhelming Image of Myself
As a Great Personage of Immense Personal Appeal
And permit me enough selflessness to find
Some living contact with my fellow players.
Prevent me, O Thespis, from savouring those moments
In which I believe I excel
And for which I shall be eulogized
By the keenest intellects of the public prints.
But rather let me "make" my moment
And glide effortlessly to the next

Devoid of self-indulgence and cramping self-esteem.
Give me the strength to forgive
Those of my fellow players
Who, using guile and evil stratagems,
Attempt to upstage me or cut-short my laughs.
Take from me the rage that I would shower
Upon the unsuspecting heads of ASMs
As they chatter in the wings before what I
(And even you, all-knowing Thespis) must admit
Is one of the truly great entrances of the evening!
Guard me against the sins of gabbling
And the desire to malinger,
The urge to dawdle and extend my part.
(For even the milk of human kindness
Should not be milked for art.)
Let my flies be fastened and my spirit-gum firm.
Let me walk upright in my rented togs
And fear not the clatter of misplaced furniture
The tardy light-cue,
The absent prop,
Or the orgiastic cough of the woman in the front row
That coincides, as if by design,
With recitation of my best line.
Let me not tarry too long at the curtain-call
Nor smile too greedily at the public's plaudits
Nor glower too rudely when they choose instead
To vent their spleen about my head.

Give me, O Thespis, the will to carry on
Despite unanimous "pans"
And the poison of friends whose backstage faces
Make me feel that being in a turkey
Is tantamount to terminal cancer.

Let me be reminded
(If indeed it be forgot)
That Art feeds off life
And that a theatre,
No matter how rich its atmosphere

Or splendid its façade,
Is surrounded by smaller edifices
Where normal men and women
Boil coffee and burn toast.

Let my life be my art
(My art never "my living")
But let me live my art
To that point of the sublime
Where I can truly say:
It is for life that I ply my art
And for the perfection of my life
That art is worth the plying
My art, the living,
My life, the dying.

Appendixes

APPENDIX 1

Exercises

The acting-exercise is the greatest challenge an actor has; greater even than the demands of the role. Using a physical invention, he is asked to conjure up something telling and creative. Very often, the exercise is devoid of any substance except that which he brings to it. A role, no matter how large or small, gives the actor some kind of framework and textual base. No matter how feeble his own personal contribution, there is always some given content to fall back on. The exercise is an invitation to unveil himself completely; to dazzle and overwhelm using his own personal stock of imagery, his own innate style, his own peculiar brand of genius. It lays bare his talent — which is why it is such a terrifying act.

Warm-Up

Actors in pairs using subtle hand-and-finger signals try to match up each other's movements. The face is kept expressionless. All emotional attitudes are conveyed by means of the hand-and-finger movements. The acting-partner, face expressionless, also using only hands and fingers, reacts.

Adjustments

One actor is seated at a table. He is utterly neutral – without character, situation or intention. A second actor enters the scene and, by playing his chosen character, situation and intention, automatically transforms the first actor into a relevant partner. The first actor, as quickly as possible, adapts to the situation imposed on him by the second actor. Before the scene is allowed to finish, a third actor enters (this being the cue for the first actor's exit) and, playing an entirely different situation, forces the second actor to adjust to a completely new set of circumstances; and so on. The most delicate point of contact – apart from the obvious adjustment of first actor to second, is the moment the third actor intrudes on the scene already in progress between actors 1 and 2. If the rhythm of the exercise is right, there is a split-second cut (without pause) between the entrance of actor 3 and the exit of actor 1. So that scenes never actually finish but unexpectedly dissolve into new ones.

The Clothesline

A couple of well-known lines from Shakespeare are chosen, i.e. "If it were done when 'tis done then 'twere well / It were done quickly" or "Is this a dagger which I see before me, / The handle toward my hand?" etc.

The Company is placed in a circle. Each actor is given one word of the line.

1. The first actor begins a definite "reading" of the line – using only the first word of the line. The second actor (on his right) attempts to pick up the colour of that line-reading and continue it on his word. The other actors, in their turn, do likewise. If successful, once the line has rippled through the entire company, it has been given a definite and comprehensible group-rendering. When unsuccessful, each actor will simply have mimicked the attitude of the first, and the result is a slightly modified repetition of one emotional colour. A good test is to re-play the line to see

if it would pass muster in any sort of interpretation of the speech. If the line has been successfully rendered, it should then be reversed – with the actor holding the last word playing out the final colour (as he ended) and everyone else obliged to recreate their original word-reading.

2. The same line is played out without emotional consistency. Each actor is obliged to choose an emotional colour as far removed as possible from the one preceding him.

3. The same line is played out with an extravagant, non-naturalistic physical action. A gesture or movement is selected – in a split second – which has no relation whatsoever to the one preceding. There should be no seconds allowed for preparation, the choice being made almost involuntarily.

4. The same line is played out with an attempt at consistent physical action. The first actor makes the first motion of a gesture. Each actor in turn is obliged to fulfil the natural tendency of that gesture. Here too, there is the danger of mimicry; that each actor will only perform a slightly varied version of the first gesture instead of allowing it to graduate naturally.

5. The Shakespearian line is played out to a familiar tune. In this variation, the first actor is allowed three or four words so that the gist of the melodic line can be recognized; the object then being for the melody to be continued – without break – from one to the other. (The bugaboo of this exercise is the unequal musical knowledge of any given company; what is an "old standard" for one actor is totally unknown to another. It is best to stick to songs with a popular national character or to indisputable old standards like "Happy Birthday to You" and "Silent Night".)

6. The line is played out in a stock accent: Irish, Scots, Brooklynese, Yiddish, etc. The first actor has only one word with which to establish the accent. Again, one should try for some kind of dramatic variety in the line so as to avoid the tendency for each actor merely displaying their version of Scots, Irish, Yiddish, etc.

7. The line is then played out only in physical movements. The aim of the group-movement should be to unify the emotional colouring of the line – (as with 1). The same pitfalls of mimicry and imitation should be avoided. The physical action of each actor should be as precise and fragmented as the words were in Exercise 1.

In all these variations, the prime requisite is the unbroken continuity of the exercise. If there are preparational gaps between words, or if the line loses its fluency of a natural speech rhythm, it is a failure. It is easy for these exercises to dwindle into isolated party-pieces which, of course, destroys the collective purposes for which they have been devised.

Death Circle
The actors form a circle and begin intoning any prayer of their own choice. The circle moves around the perimeter of the room. At some point on that perimeter, a white mark has been painted. On a signal, the praying and circling stops abruptly. Whoever has reached the white mark is obliged to die in some way of his own choosing. The rhythm, style and manner of his death is entirely up to the actor – hence it can be straight, comic, abrupt, elongated or whatever. No two actors may perform the same death. The dead actor remains on the floor until the entire group dies.

Howdown
The company forms a circle. A leader is selected, and he or she begins to clap out a rhythm which the others quickly duplicate, syncopate and embellish. An actor steps into the centre of the circle and begins performing a speech from the play – adjusting the rhythm of his delivery to the tempo of the group's clapping. As the clapping tempo changes (and the changes should not simply go from fast to slow, but contain differences of volume, texture and dramatic character), the actor changes his speech accordingly. As soon as he feels he has had enough, without interruption, he resumes his place in the circle cueing another actor into his place into the centre. Throughout the exercise, the object is for the actor to perform the group will. His interpretation is entirely regulated by the changes occurring in the tempi of the group. Eventually, the leader can be forsaken altogether, and the group should be able to ring its changes by itself. When this can be brought about smoothly, it indicates a highly developed sense of group contact.

Macbeth Stew
Different scenes from the play are divided between five couples. The scenes should be short, compact and, wherever possible, self-

sufficient, i.e. the Malcolm–Macduff Scene (IV.3), the Conspiracy Scene between Macbeth and Lady Macbeth (I.7), Banquo and Macbeth (III.1) etc. Since several scenes may include Macbeth, he should be played by as many different actors as is feasible.

1. The scenes are played out straight.
2. The scenes are conditioned by unrelated actions (i.e. Macbeth and Lady Macbeth playing tennis, taking ballet instructions, doing the dishes, etc.) with the scene's original intentions observed as faithfully as possible.
3. The scenes, with unrelated physical business, are played so that the intentions are radically changed, that is, in accordance with the dictates of the new business (i.e. Macbeth petulant at having to wash while Lady Macbeth dries; Lady Macbeth irritated by Macbeth's ineptitude at ballet-instructions, etc.).
4. On a signal, the couples playing their scenes simultaneously, split up and begin playing their scenes with other characters. Now a Lady Macbeth may be playing her Conspiracy Scene with a Macduff who is playing his Testing Scene. The more dominant physical action dominates the scene, and the words become nothing more than a sound-cover for sub-textual meanings wholly unrelated to the text (i.e. Macduff, still using the words of his original scene, may be playing the henpecked husband of a domineering wife; Macduff, using his original text, may be urged to murder by a shrewish Lady Macbeth, etc.).
5. Signals are then given in quick succession with only one or two minutes' pause between. On each signal, characters break away from their original partners, and quickly match up with another; any other. As they do so, their scene automatically changes its action, attitude and intention. In every case the more dominant idea should be allowed to prevail; the playing-partner adapting as quickly as possible.

The reason for fracturing a Shakespearian scene – altering the original meaning of its text but keeping the words intact, complicating its situation with incongruous business and unrelated acting-partners, is to compel actors to control both disparate and multiple elements. One part of the actor's techniques is dealing with words, another with feelings, a third with actions, a fourth with contact, and all the while, all these elements are shifting, changing, reversing, returning. The overall effect, from the audience's standpoint, is simultaneity, but within this jumble of words and actions, the actor is the regulator of a highly sophisticated piece of equipment: himself. Therefore, jumbled as it certainly is, it is never unaccountable chaos; unless of course, the actor sinks beneath the multiple pressures. When successful, it is a rich fusion of several elements which, like the components of a printing-press, create an impression of impossible complexity and yet, when the printing-press slows down, are individually recognizable.

These kinds of exercises deal with the actor as mechanism because the human being which animates the actor *is* a mechanism; just as theatre is the synthesis of many mechanisms. The danger is that the performance of these mechanisms produces a purely *mechanistic* effect – which of course has nothing to do with the intentions of art. In such a case, it would be as if the complicated machinery of the printing-press was functioning only to demonstrate the facility of its equipment, without actually printing anything. It is important that the end for which these mechanisms are being lubricated is always kept in mind; so that exercises never *lose* themselves in displays of technique, but *utilize* technique to express more than could be expressed if technique were not that highly sophisticated.

The actor who complains he is being treated like a robot is often bawling for the self-indulgence of the monocelled performer. Give me my lines and my moves, cries his sub-text, and I will give you a thundering exhibition of my immovable clichés. If there were no other benefit to these exercises it would be sufficient that they rob the actor of the complacency which type-casting and artistic sloth engender in his being. The actor is always asking for a "challenge" until he actually gets one; then you realize what he meant was a big, showy part for himself.

Male-Female
A male actor chooses a typical female situation (i.e. instruction on childbirth, trying on lingerie, receiving beauty-parlour treatment) and plays it out in his own character but with all the appropriate female choices. There should be no attempt at phoney female voices or female parody. The object of the exercise is for the male to

assimilate the female situation as faithfully as possible in his own character.

Multiples
Best performed with a group of twelve. All standing in a circle.

1ST ACTOR: Lays down a basic rhythmic beat (not a melody) which serves as a bass-accompaniment to the exercise.

2ND ACTOR: Augments this beat with a rhythm of his own which, in range and texture, is as dissimilar as possible but still fits into the given rhythm.

3RD ACTOR: Does likewise.

4TH ACTOR: Does likewise.

5TH ACTOR: Chooses the name of a disease and performs that rhythmically, i.e. "laryngitis" – broken down into sound-components: *lah*-ryn-gi-tis, lah-*ryn*-gi-tis, lah-ryn-*gi*-tis, etc.

6TH ACTOR: Continually repeats four bars of a popular song.

7TH ACTOR: Plays out an advertisement slogan augmenting the group-rhythm: "Persil Washes Whiter", "Guiness is Good for You", "Keep Britain Tidy", etc.

8TH ACTOR: Punctuates group-rhythm with a cry. No matter how searing the cry, it must – in some way – fit into the collective rhythm and must never be rhythmically arbitrary.

9TH ACTOR: *Using* only plosives, non-vocalized sounds, adds to the collective rhythm.

10TH ACTOR: Using his body as an instrument, claps out a beat which fits into the collective rhythm.

11TH ACTOR: Using sharp, rhythmic gestures, adds movements that fits into the collective rhythm.

12TH ACTOR: Begins to tell the story of his life in a dry, matter-of-fact, conventional style.

NB The group-rhythm must never be imitative but always complementary: that is, everyone's contribution, by being tonally or texturally different from what has gone before, must enrich the overall texture of the whole.

Once the group-rhythm is under way, the director uses the Auto-biographist (12th Actor) as a soloist, relegating everyone else to the level of accompaniment. He conducts the Auto-biographist to the centre and signals for the background actors to subside in volume. In this way, the soloist's biography becomes the main-line of the exercise; the others providing a dulled, but discernible, repeated accompaniment. Ideally, they are listening to the soloist while performing their own repeated contributions. Then the conductor (director) signals to another actor to become the Auto-biographist – soloist. The new Auto-biographist abandons his own rhythmic contribution and begins telling the story of his life while the previous Auto-biographist (12th Actor) retires to the background still speaking his Auto-biography, but now as part of the dulled accompaniment. This process continues until all have become Auto-biographists. (During the soloists' performance, the director–conductor regulates the group's performance as he wishes – changing tempi and dynamics.)

Towards the end of the exercise, soloists, instead of being waved into the background, remain in the centre telling their stories while other soloists are signalled in. Eventually, there are four or five auto-biographies being spoken simultaneously; then eight, nine, ten, etc. Eventually, everyone is speaking their auto-biography at the same time. Again, the din is a concentration factor, and the object is to retain the line of one's story in the midst of the jumble of speech on every side.

Help Play

The room is littered with numerous obstacles; overturned chairs, banana-peels, balls, heavy equipment, trays of water, etc. One set of actors (the Movers) are blindfolded; alongside them a second set of actors (the Helpers). The Helpers' job is to guide the Movers from one end of the room to the other without the Movers colliding with any of the obstacles. This is done by the Helpers whispering instructions into the ears of the Movers. If there are six or seven people performing the exercise at the same time, the din of everyone talking at once is a useful complicating factor encouraging greater concentration. Once the Movers have successfully traversed the room, they become the Helpers and vice versa.

Soliloquy

The actor is placed on a stage, or in the centre of the room with a single spotlight on him as isolated from the others as possible. Let us say his name is John Doe.

Alexis Kanner as Hamlet, Jonathan Burn as Fortinbras, in the first version of *Hamlet* adapted by Marowitz and directed by Charles Marowitz and Peter Brook for the "Theatre of Cruelty" at LAMDA, 1963
(*Photo Michael Hardy*)

Left to right, Jonathan Burn, Glenda Jackson and Susan Williams in a piece for the "Theatre of Cruelty" at LAMDA, 1963
(*Photo Michael Hardy*)

Glenda Jackson, *centre*, in a "Theatre of Cruelty" production, 1963
(*Photo Michael Hardy*)

Glenda Jackson and Alexis Kanner in a LAMDA "Theatre of Cruelty"
production, 1963   (*Photo Michael Hardy*)

The Royal Shakespeare Company Experimental Group in Scene 2 of
The Screens by Genet, a production by Brook and Marowitz, 1963
(*Photo Morris Newcombe*)

The Royal Shakespeare
Company in *Marat/Sade*
by Weiss, directed by Peter
Brook, 1965: *above,* Patrick
Magee and Glenda Jackson;
below, left to right, Freddie
Jones, Patrick Magee, Hugh
Sullivan, Jeannett Landis,
Jonathan Burn, Guy Gordon
(*By permission of the Governors
of the Royal Shakespeare
Theatre, Stratford-upon-Avon*)

He is then asked to imagine that he is a character in a play. His character's name is his own, John Doe; the title of his play is *The Life of John Doe*. During the course of this "play", he comes centre-stage and he begins a soliloquy, unburdening his heart and mind to the audience and using as his springboard, the events of his present day. He begins (everyone begins in the same way) with the words, "What a day . . ." He then goes on to explore the feelings produced by the day's events, the events themselves, everything and anything relating to his present mood. The object is to discover what that mood is – how he is actually feeling that day – and to use his recollections to define that mood without exaggeration or dramatization.

Before the exercise, it should be stressed that the object is not for the actor to indulge in day-dreams or private ramblings, but to catch the dominant quality of the day's mood and to recreate it organically using selected material from his immediate experience; to unify what may be a jumble of contradictory feelings into one, unified state of being: (i.e. Hamlet's philosophic melancholy in "To be or not to be", his sense of personal inadequacy in "How all occasions do inform against me", his expression of self-disgust and impotence in "O, that this too too solid flesh would melt", etc.).

When the mood has been successfully captured, the exercise should be stopped. After several actors have performed the exercise, other actors should be selected to re-create the moods most effectively evoked using different personal material. (i.e. a convincing sense of personal futility has been created by a particular actor; another has managed to create a sense of irrational contentment with life. The second actor is awarded the mood of the first and asked to summon up images from another part of his life to evoke a mood he doesn't feel at the moment; the first actor is assigned the mood of the second actor, etc.)

Oratorio

(A collage-Exercise)

Each member of the group is given a lecture-title (i.e. My Most Embarrassing Moment, My First Sexual Experience, Why Britain Needs Fascism, How to Change a Tyre, How to Make a Mushroom Omelette, The Story of My Life, Why Karl Marx and Abe Lincoln Were One and the Same Person, etc.). As the group slowly circles the room, each actor is encouraged to work up (mentally) material for his or her lecture, the condition being that he or she must speak convincingly on whatever subject is designated – whether or not they agree with the thesis.

They are then instructed that as soon as the director taps a particular person, that person using a strong, oratorical voice, begins their lecture. However, as soon as they hear another person giving their lecture (as a result of another tap by the director), the first person halts their speech in mid-sentence or mid-syllable but when the first speaker is tapped again, he or she must resume their lecture at precisely the point where they cut off – in mid-sentence or mid-syllable. When they hear yet another person begin their lecture, they must again cut out. The arbitrary connections between one actor's speech and another is regulated by the director tapping various speakers – obviously trying for maximum contrast of speeches (i.e. intimate sexual descriptions intercut with instructions on how to change a tyre, a political harangue mingled with descriptions of cake recipes, etc.).

At a certain point in the exercise, after most people have had an opportunity to begin their lectures and speak for about a half-minute or more, the director encourages the Speakers (who are still circling the room slowly as they orate) all to speak at once, viz., deliver their lectures as if alone, and addressing a lecture-audience, but in fact, simultaneous with every other person in the exercise.

Once the entire group is talking together, the director, again using judicious taps, begins to cut out one speaker after another – until three or four speakers are speaking simultaneously; gradually, he subtracts voice after voice, until only one speaker is speaking – then he returns to the earlier convention tapping various people in turn, creating collage out of the various lectures – but now in somewhat shorter bursts.

The speakers are then assembled into one group – like the members of an orchestra. It is explained that there is now going to be a concert with the director acting as conductor and the actors serving as musicians – however, instead of essaying music, the speakers will be performing the material presented in their lectures. Not sung but spoken. Not even spoken exactly, but intoned and "performed" according to the tempo and dynamics laid down by the Conductor. If he wants a slow tempo, he conducts one; if he wants a fast one, he accelerates it. If he wants lyricism, he asks for it, facially and posturally, the way conductors do. If he wants power and bombast from his orchestra, he has to convey that to them – as a conductor would – using his own means of expression. His orchestra, using the same lecture-material they have just performed in the earlier exercise (starting from the beginning of their talk and repeating verbatim as best they can) must give the conductor what he wants – in terms of tempi, dynamics and expression.

Once the director has demonstrated how to conduct the words as music, he should allow as many actors as is feasible to become conductors in their own right. Gradually, new permutations will develop. A conductor can have one soloist at the side : working with or against the orchestra; then two soloists; then a small grouping of five or six. One Speaker can then be turned into a prima-ballerina and when she is given her cue by the Conductor, she must dance her lecture in the tempo and with the feelings demanded of her by the new Conductor. Three girls can become a can-can ensemble; a boy and girl can perform their lectures in ballroom position. One actor can be turned into a Flamenco dancer or a Jazz-dancer. Whatever the nature of the soloist or soloists, they must, in addition to dancing their parts, continue to convey their lecture according to the dictates of the Conductor. The Conductor, for his part, must regulate his various orchestral components as best he can – and with the maximum variety.

Towards the close of this exercise, the "Orchestra" can be divided in three or four smaller groups, each with their own conductor. The groups, after having been static, can begin to move across the room – again, led by the rhythmic whims of their particular Conductor. When this exercise reaches a state of unbearable pandemonium, it should be allowed to finish, but it is best to keep at it until a certain kind of group frenzy has been created – something the very opposite of the formal lectures performed by the actors in their initial addresses. The final "sound" of the exercise should be as far removed from the sound of spoken language as possible.

The Single Ticket

All flights have been grounded. There is one available seat on a special flight from London to New York. Because of this unique situation, the airline has decided to interview those persons wishing to obtain the flight. They will then decide to whom the single ticket should be awarded.

Each actor, devising his own reasons for having to fly to New York, is interviewed by an airline representative. The object of the exercise is twofold: (a) to devise persuasive reasons in order to obtain the ticket and (b) to create in the interview the most plausible and engrossing scene possible.

The Unsuitable Applicant

The following advert has appeared in *The Times* of London: "Wanted: A Gentleman's gentleman: A well-spoken, well-educated, genteel person with poise and breeding to be valet to an old and respected peer of the realm. Must possess all refinements, be conversant with several languages and, above all, tactful and courteous."

Actors are encouraged to devise characters as far removed from this description as possible to apply for this appointment. Character choices can be as extravagant as one chooses, so long as the extravagance can be sustained during the course of the interview to which each character comes in turn. The interviewer, like the noble lord who employs him, should be a sterling representative of the upper class.

Greetings

The actor chooses an attitude to the person greeted and works up a short background relationship which only he knows. The "greeting" consists of only a few words, a "hello", a handshake perhaps, a wave of the hand – whatever is appropriate to the choice. After the exercise, the company tries to interpret the intent behind the greeting and to guess what some of the background choices might be.

Examples:

Greeting an old and dear friend. Someone you haven't seen for years; someone you have been looking forward to for a long time.

Greeting your immediate superior at work. Someone you despise and would like to destroy but to whom you must always be amiable and polite if you are to remain in your present employment.

Greeting someone you suspect to be a deadly enemy; someone

whom you feel would just as soon stab you in the back as smile at you.

Greeting someone you have always read about and silently revered, and of whom you have built up a very glamorous image. Being encountered at a social occasion.

Greeting someone with whom you have had a long and intense affair but of whom you have now grown tired.

Greeting someone you immensely enjoy; someone who always makes you laugh and shows you a good time.

Greeting someone so celebrated it awes you; someone whose achievement is so formidable that beside him, you feel small and insignificant.

Greeting someone very aged and decrepit about whom you feel a burdensome responsibility. Someone who relies on you and has begun to take you for granted, and who is unaware of the oppressiveness you feel in his presence.

In all of these Greetings, the person greeted must be as neutral as possible, so that the tenor of your greeting may determine his character. A variation on this is for the exercise to be played in pairs, with your partner previously genned up on the character who inspires the greeting.

Text-Tests

1. Type out an unfamiliar Shakespearian speech deleting all punctuation so that it becomes an unbroken ream of verse. Then give it to an actor and have him punctuate it in his delivery.
2. Take a fully punctuated Shakespearian speech and have an actor perform it observing the punctuation as faithfully as possible. Let the other actors call out commas, semi-colons, hyphens, full-stops, etc. as they think they occur.
3. Take a fully punctuated Shakespearian speech and perform it speaking all the punctuation-marks. Play the same speech again and, wherever a piece-of-punctuation occurs, have the actor perform a movement which corresponds to the comma, the colon, the hyphen, the full-stop, etc., giving each punctuation-movement the sweep and duration required by the text.
4. Take a piece of prose and force it into iambic pentameter.

5. Take a piece of verse and force it into a prose-rhythm.
6. Take the copy of an advertisement from a newspaper or magazine and re-structure it into verse.
7. Take a telephone-directory and, linking the names together as your text, tell a story which is:

    (a) A mystery-thriller
    (b) A romantic love-tale
    (c) A children's fairy-tale
    (d) A public announcement
    (e) A blow-by-blow description of a boxing-bout or a lap-by-lap account of a horse-race
    (f) A funeral oration
    (g) A militant political address,
       etc.

APPENDIX 2

Notes on "The Theatre of Cruelty"

In the fall of 1963, Peter Brook and I formed an experimental group affiliated with the Royal Shakespeare Company. The intention was to explore certain problems of acting and stagecraft in laboratory conditions, without the commercial pressures of public performance. The following account is based on notes and jottings from that period, as well as reflections after the event.

THE AUDITIONS

Since we weren't casting any particular play and therefore weren't on the lookout for any *types*, and since our main concern was to find actors who were open, adaptable, and ready to rush in where rigid pros fear to tread, it was necessary to devise a completely new audition technique. I decided to do away with those murky soliloquies where a single actor pulsating with suppressed but crippling hysteria gets up and reels off the same speech he has been carting around since drama school. The auditions were collective; anywhere from eight to ten actors working together for at least an hour. The audition was broken up in the following ways:

Disrupted Set-Piece:
The actor is asked to perform his two-minute set-piece in his own way, without suggestions or interference. Once he has done this, he is given a new character and a new situation and asked to play these, still retaining the text of his original speech. (An actor who comes along with "To be or not to be . . ." is asked to play King Lear in the death scene or Romeo in the balcony scene *through* the Hamlet text.) The task is for the actor to throw himself into a completely different set of circumstances (to improvise) and yet to retain control over his original text (to operate formally). Once the actor has managed to create a smattering of the new character and the new situation, he is given yet another character and a different situation (a barrow-salesman on a market-day, a political candidate standing for re-election), until he has three balls to juggle at once: (1) his original choice; (2) the first variation; (3) the second variation. The actor is then given cue-words which refer to each of his characters, and he is asked to switch rapidly among the three different situations without breaking the flow of his original text.

Text and Sub-Text:
The actor is given a piece of nonsense-text. There is no discernible character or situation. The actor makes of it whatever he can, but he is obliged to use the given words. (This enabled us to discover how the actor, on the most elementary level, coped with language – where his natural instincts led him. It is like a Rorschach test with words instead of ink-blots.)

Object Associations:
An object is thrown out on to the stage – a toy shovel, for instance. The actor proceeds to build up a scene (in mime only) using the shovel. When something has begun to develop, when the actor feels he is finally *on* to something, another object, entirely unrelated (a briefcase, a shoe-horn, a telephone-directory, a plant) is thrown out

and the actor is obliged either to create a completely new scene or develop a bridge between the unrelated objects.

Discontinuous Improvisations:
An actor performing a simple, recognizable action (digging, golfing, wall-papering, exercising) enters. The others choose actions which relate to that actor's choice and a scene (with words) develops. A enters digging with a shovel; B mimes a pneumatic drill; C grabs a wheelbarrow; D becomes a works-supervisor checking his stopwatch. Then a new actor enters performing a completely unrelated action (making lyrical pliés), the other actors adapt to the new action as quickly as possible. (One begins to *plier*, another, Martha Graham-like, rolls his body into a ball; a third begins marking time with a stick.) As each new situation is perceived and developed, another one, as far removed as possible, is begun. Eventually, three separate teams are chosen – each with its own built-in changes – and these three groups, working simultaneously, weave among as many as twelve different situations. The cleanliness of the changes is what counts, also the rapidity with which actors cotton on to the changed situation. The scenes themselves are, of necessity, superficial, but the object is not to create substantial, well-sinewed improvisations, but merely to follow up dramatic leads as quickly as they present themselves.

THE FIRST COMPANY

Out of about fifty actors a dozen were selected, and then presented to Brook for approval. (Ironically, there was a slight hassle only in the case of Glenda Jackson, over whom Brook took some convincing. She turned out to be – along with Alexis Kanner – one of the two most resourceful members of the group.)

The average age of the group was twenty-four. Only one member was over thirty, and most were just over twenty. The backgrounds were television, drama-school, a minimal amount of repertory, no West End experience to speak of. The general formation was naturalistic – a grounding in Stanislavsky techniques as attenuated and distorted by English drama schools. I felt the need to start from scratch, to plunge the whole company into elementary Method

exercises before totally demolishing the Stanislavsky ethic. Brook
disagreed. He felt the level of proficiency was high enough to tackle
the new work directly. I thought this a mistake because Stanislavsky
was the grammar out of which we were going to build a completely
different syntax and I wanted the basis to be sound before shifting it.
It is difficult to say, in retrospect, whether we were right or wrong
in plunging a group of twelve young actors and actresses into the
swirling water of Artaudian theory, but, of course, there was the
time-factor. We had only twelve weeks for training and a preliminary workshop performance. We worked in a small church hall
behind the Royal Court Theatre in Sloane Square; a bare, wooden
room littered with Brownie posters and the relics of ancient whist-
drives. It was a long day, beginning at 10 a.m. and ending at 6 p.m.
Each night Brook and I consulted by phone about the objectives of
the next day's session, then I sat down and devised the exercises
which made up the next day's work. My notes of these sessions
are not chronological, and so what follows is in no particular
order.

Introduction to Sounds:
On the very first day of work, before the actors had properly met
each other and without Brook or me delivering any orientation
lectures, the actors were handed objects: boxes, bangers, scrapers,
vessels, sticks, etc. Each actor had something or other to bang with,
and something or other to bang on. They were then asked to explore
the range of their *instrument* (the sound the thin end of a ladle made
on a tin can; the sound the tin can made against the floor, muted with
one palm, held suspended, in two hands, tucked inside a sweater,
rapped with the knuckle instead of the ladle, with the forehead
instead of the knuckle, the elbow instead of the forehead . . .). Once
the range of the instrument had been explored, a series of rhythms
were rapped out. Some of these were then varied while others remained the same; some were accelerated while others were slowed
down; there were combinations of twos and threes; dialogues
between broomhandles and empty crates; scenes from *Romeo
and Juliet* played out between metallic tinkles and bass percussions;
mob violence with soapcrates and pitched battles with tennis
rackets.
        Eventually *rhythm*, a generalized and over-used word in the

theatre, got re-defined in exact, physical terms. Not only did actors experience the basic changes of rhythm – slow, fast, moderate – but the endless combinations and counterpoints that rhythms were capable of. Shortly, the same attitude the actors had taken to their objects was applied to their voices and bodies. This was a tortuous adjustment, and one was always fighting the primordial instinct in English actors that believes the voice is the medium for *good speech*, *projection*, and *resonance*, the carrier of the theatrical "message", and the body a useful but secondary adjunct. Little by little, we insinuated the idea that the voice could produce sounds other than grammatical combinations of the alphabet, and that the body, set free, could begin to enunciate a language which went beyond text, beyond sub-text, beyond psychological implication and beyond monkey-see-monkey-do facsimiles of social behaviourism. And most important of all, that these sounds and moves could communicate feelings and ideas.

Sound-and-Movement Similes:
EXERCISE: You come back to your apartment after a hard day's work. Enter, take off your coat, hang it up, pour yourself a drink and sit down at the table. On the table is a letter which you suddenly notice. You put down the drink, open the letter and begin to read. Depending on what the contents trigger off, express this state using only a sound and a movement. (Previous to the exercise, a simple piece of emotionally charged information has been prepared in each letter, i.e. "We regret to inform you your entire family has been destroyed in a fire that has swept the city", "I have been watching you from afar for days, unable to come up and confess that I am passionately in love with you", or "I am pleased to inform you you have just won £300,000 in the Pools", "I have been watching your movements for days. Before this week is out, you will be dead", or "The citizens of our city have unanimously voted to ask you to become the next candidate for Mayor", etc.)

The moments in the exercise leading up to the final beat are entirely naturalistic, but the final beat is an externalized expression of the character's inner state and totally non-naturalistic. At first, all the choices were commonplace. People jumped for joy, fell into weeping, bolted upwards with surprise, stamped with rage. When none of these simple expressions was acceptable, the actors began to realize the nature of the exercise. With all their naturalistic choices dismissed out of hand, they had to go in search of a more stylized means of communication. Eventually, the choices became more imaginative. Sounds were created which had the resonance of wounded animals; of pre-historic creatures being slain by atomic weapons. Movements became stark and unpredictable. Actors began to use the chairs and tables as sculptural objects instead of functional furniture. Facial expressions, under the pressure of extended sounds, began to resemble Javanese masks and Zen sculpture. But once the actors realized what we were after, some of them began to select an arbitrary sound or movement, effective in itself but unrelated to the emotional state growing out of the exercise. Very quickly, frighteningly quickly, actors became as glib with non-naturalistic sounds and movements as they were with stock, dramatic clichés. One wondered if Artaud's idealized theatre ever were established whether, in five or ten years, it too would not become as practised and cliché-ridden as the present-day Comédie Française, or the West End.

Discontinuity:

One of the main objects behind the work was to create a discontinuous style of acting; that is, a style which corresponded to the broken and fragmentary way in which most people experience contemporary reality. Life today (I am not philosophizing, merely trying to illustrate) is very much like the front page of a daily newspaper. The eye jumps from one story to another; from one geographical location to another; from one mood to another. A fire in Hoboken; an election in Paris; a coronation in Sweden; a rape in London; comedy, passion, ceremony, trivia — all flooding one's consciousness almost simultaneously. The actor, however, through years of training and centuries of tradition, moves stolidly from point A to point B to point C. His character is *established*, his relationships *develop*; his plot thickens and his conflicts resolve. In short, he plods on in his Aristotelian way, perpetuating the stock jargon of drama and the arbitrary time-system of the conventional theatre.

To break the progressive-logical-beginning-middle-and-end syndrome, one uses improvisation (personal and organic material rather than theatrical *données*) and uses it simply as rhythmic matter.

EXERCISE: The life of a character is briefly built up. X is an out-of-work writer.

Scene 1: His landlady asks him for rent which is months in arrears.

Scene 2: His girl-friend wants to know when they're going to get married.

Scene 3: His father urges him to give up writing and take a job with a firm.

Scene 4: His pub-crony exhorts him to come out, have a drink, and forget his troubles.

Scene 5: His school-friend drops in and wants to re-live old times.

Scene 6: An insurance salesman persistently tries to push an unwanted policy on him.

Each scene is built up independently for five or ten minutes; just long enough for it to have a little meat, but not long enough to develop any real sinew. Then X is placed in the centre of the room and each character – on cue – resumes his scene with him. The scenes, all unrelated except that they all centre around the same main character, follow hard upon each other. With the addition of each new scene, X quickly adapts to the changed situation, the different relationship. Eventually, three and four scenes are being played at once. Soon all are being played simultaneously. At a point, the exercise becomes unbearable and impossible, but before that point, X and his fellow actors have experienced a frantic sense of discontinuity that just begins to convey the complexities to which any, even the simplest, sensibility is prone.

A COLLAGE-*HAMLET*

A couple of years before the Royal Shakespeare Experimental Group, I had invited Brook along to a play I was doing at the In-Stage studio-theatre at Fitzroy Square. It was a short play by Lionel Abel called *A Little Something for the Maid*. Originally intended for radio, it consisted of a series of short, discontinuous scenes in which the female character became, by turns, everybody in the male character's life: wife, sweetheart, charlady, male-employer, secretary, mother, etc. Discussing it afterwards, Brook had said it would be fascinating to see *Hamlet* played that way, re-shuffled like a deck of familiar cards. A year and a half later, Brook's idea still knocking around in my head, I sat down to restructure Shakespeare's play.

The idea of the LAMDA *Hamlet* was to condense the play into about twenty minutes, without relying on narrative. This was on the assumption that everyone knew *Hamlet*, even those people who hadn't read or seen it; that there was a smear of Hamlet in everyone's collective unconscious and that it was possible to predicate a performance on that mythic smear.

The play was spliced up into a collage with lines juxtaposed, sequences rearranged, characters dropped or blended, and the entire thing played out in fragments which appeared like subliminal flashes out of Hamlet's life. In every case I used Shakespeare's words, although radically rearranged.

Of all the discontinuity exercises, this had the firmest foundation, as all the actors knew the original play and therefore had an emotional and narrative frame of reference. The first version was essentially a clever exercise in Burroughs-like cut-ups. In the later, expanded 85-minute version which played in Germany, Italy, and later London, the style was better assimilated, the play had more intellectual content and was at the service of a clear-cut interpretation.

CONTACT

The building of company-sense demands the construction of those delicate vertebrae and interconnecting tissues that transform an aggregation of actors into an ensemble. A protracted period of togetherness (at a rep, for instance) creates an accidental union between people, but this isn't the same thing as actors coiled and sprung in relation to one another – poised in such a way that a move from one creates a tremor from another; an impulse from a third, an immediate chain-reaction. Contact doesn't mean staring in the eyes of your fellow-actor for all you're worth. It means being so well tuned in that you can see him without looking. It means, in rare cases, being linked by a group rhythm which is regulated almost physiologically – by blood circulation or heart palpitation. It is the sort of thing that exists between certain kith and kin; certain husbands and wives; certain kinds of lovers or bitter enemies.

Group Interview:
EXERCISE : A is a social outcast who has spent some time in jail. He has now been released and is being interviewed for a routine job by an interviewer for a large firm who knows his background but is prepared to consider him for employment. A needs the job, hates the idea of being patronized, and is torn between ingratiating himself and venting his hostilities. The rest of the group (sixteen actors) are personality-adjuncts of A. B represents his social hostility; C, his economic need; D, his attempt to conform; E, his rebellious nature; F, his innate cowardice; G, his suppressed social ambition; H, his fantasy-image of himself as a Great Man, and so on. None of A's personality extensions initiate any material in the scene. They speak only as and when A replies to the Interviewer's questions, and their response is determined entirely by what A actually says and what they glean from the way he says it. Depending on those replies, one or another of A's personality adjuncts take prominence. But with every response, all sixteen actors pick up, echo, modify, or extend A's replies in the scene.

> INTERVIEWER. Do you think you would be happy in this job?
> A. Oh yes . . . I think I'd like it very much.
> B, *viciously.* Who wants to know?
> C, *pleadingly.* Just try me out for a week, you'll see.
> H, *imperiously.* I'll be sitting behind that desk in a month's time.
> D, *tentatively.* Could I wear a suit like that, I wonder?
> F, *fretfully.* I wonder whether I'm going to be kicked out of this office.
> E, *aggressively.* I'd love to put my fist in your eye.

The exercise musters an agonizing degree of attention and, as each actor must speak simultaneously with A, compels actors to grasp implications and innuendoes instead of responding mechanically to word-cues. In other words, it forces actors to cope with sub-text, and to recognize top-text only as a kind of tackle that leads down to the underwater world where all the essential action lies.

Improvs and Essentials:

There was a good deal of conventional improvisation (built up on actions and reducible to beats), but the more useful work came from variations and extensions of the stock Method approach. For instance: after a scene was played, the actor was asked to divide the improv into three units, and to give a line-title to each unit. Once this was accomplished and it was generally agreed that the line-titles were appropriate to the situation just played, the scene was re-played in its entirety with the actors using only their three line-titles as dialogue. Then the actor was asked to choose only one word from each of the three line-titles, and the scene was played a third time with the sound components of those words serving exclusively as the dialogue. Then (and only then) the actor could choose a sound which accurately reflected the main quality of his scene and play the scene for a final time, using variations of that sound. The playing in sound invariably prompted a non-naturalistic use of movement, and it was fascinating to see how, once the situation had been ground down to basic impulses, the movement graphically expressed the true intentions behind the scene.

Example: Scene – A wants to break off long-standing affair with his girl-friend, B. He now realizes he does not love her, and it would be lunacy to marry. B, however, has become helplessly attached to A and cannot bear the idea of parting. She tries desperately to maintain the relationship.

Scene Breakdown in Terms of Line-Titles: First Replay.

Boy 1. I want to break off this affair.

2. I want to be as kind as possible.

3. I won't be persuaded to change my mind.

Girl 1. I want to keep my hold on A.

2. I want to reason with him so as to change his mind.

3. I refuse to be hurt.

Second Replay: Essential words.

Boy. Break
      Kind
      Won't

Girl. Keep
      Reason
      Refuse

Third Replay: Sounds.

Boy. Ey-ayeOoghn

Girl. Eey-zoohz

(The sounds are fluid and free, merely *based on* the vowels and consonants of the essential words.)

Changing Gears:

Three actors, A, B, and C, are given cue-sounds (a bell for one, a buzzer for the second, a gong for the third). When A hears his cue, he initiates a scene; B and C, adapting themselves to A's choice, enter into the situation as quickly as possible. After two or three minutes, when the scene is either approaching a highpoint or running down because of lack of invention, B is given his cue. B suddenly leaps into a completely new situation, entirely unrelated to the one preceding; A and C adapt themselves immediately. Short development, then C is cued, another unrelated scene, the others adapt again, etc.

As important as the actual material thrown up by the scene is the moment chosen for breaking it and beginning another. There is a moment in almost every improvisation where things reach a head and are moving quickly towards a resolution. If one can trigger off the new scene just at that moment, the actor's emergency equipment is instinctively brought into play. Improvisations like these feed on (and sometimes are destroyed by) their sense of danger. There is an inescapable imperative forced on the actors. They must think and act with lightning speed. They know that within a seven or ten minute period, they have to devise as many as five or six different situations, and they soon discover they cannot cheat by planning ahead, because a pre-arranged choice is immediately apparent – as is the instinctively appropriate choice which could not have come from anywhere else but the given circumstances. It brings into play a quality that actors tend to think they do not possess: the ability to associate freely and without regard to fixed character or logical consistency. For me, the great eye-opener in this exercise was how, under the pressure of changing gears, actors who had never heard of surrealism, were able to make the most stunning surrealist choices; and actors who claimed to have no sense of humour, suddenly found themselves dipping into deep wells of fantasy and absurdity that lay on the threshold of their consciousness. Choices which, if actors had time to deliberate over them, would never be made, or would be doctored or modified, leaped out with astonishing clarity and boldness.

Speak with Paints:

EXERCISE: You have just come out of your flat, locked the door, and put the key in your pocket. You walk over to the elevator and ring. Casually you look through your newspaper as you wait for the elevator to arrive. On a sound-cue, the elevator arrives, the doors slide open and in the elevator you discover a completely unexpected person towards whom you have a strong, specific attitude of one sort or another. (The actor decides background beforehand.) At that instant, you rush to the easel and immediately express that attitude in paints.

As in the similar exercise with the Letter, the most delicate moment in the exercise is the one in which the actor confronts his stranger and moves to express his attitude. If you can organically link yourself to the next, the result is clean and communicative. If there is even a second's hesitation, the result is self-conscious, unnatural, and merely *illustrated*. A later version of this exercise, which proved more successful, was for the actor to play out an improvisation with the stranger in which the chosen attitude was actually manifest, then to have an interim scene inside the flat, followed by the exercise situation. Otherwise, the actor is working too exclusively from a mental frame of reference.

At first, the paintings were sloppy and crude. On the third and fourth repeat, they were almost artistic, in that they were meaningful, impressionistic blotches which *did* suggest an internal state, interpretable by the other group-members. The paint exercise was used directly in Artaud's *The Spurt of Blood*, by author's direction in *The Screens*, and in a more sophisticated version in the *Marat/Sade*. (The red, blue, and white paint sequences in *Marat/Sade* stem from a similar effect in Brook's production of *Titus Andronicus*, where Vivien Leigh used an unfurled red ribbon to symbolize the flow of blood.)

REFORMS: One must assume that Artaud's "fragile, fluctuating centre that forms never reach" refers to states beyond the reach of *linguistic* forms, but accessible by other means. Otherwise it is soapy mysticism. The potential superiority of an Artaudian theatre –

compared even to an overhauled and much-improved realistic theatre – lies in the fact that its language is not yet discovered, therefore not yet tarnished and empty. The danger is that a backlog of five centuries filled with verbal debris may never enable it to hit bedrock. Or to put it even more pessimistically: the actor's social and psychological conditioning is both the main obstacle to be removed, and the one factor which is immovable.

ACTORS AND ACTORS

The hallmark of a good actor is his attitude towards change. Most actors make their decisions in the first stages of rehearsal, chart the shortest distance between two points and then proceed in a straight line. For these, the rehearsal period is a tunnel with light on one end and light on the other, and a great stretch of darkness in the middle. Another sort of actor retains the ability to re-think and re-organize his role throughout. He follows every lead and yields to every permutation, and isn't put off by detours and secondary routes. He may take longer to arrive but when he does, he brings a better-rounded result.

This attitude towards change almost distinguishes two separate breeds of actor, and in England today these breeds intermingle in almost every company. It is too sweeping to designate one *traditional*, and the other *modern*, but there is a grain of truth in that distinction – those actors who have passed through the Royal Court, Theatre Workshop, and the ferment of the past ten years tend to have a more open attitude than can be found among the academy-bred, rep-orientated actors of an older formation. Each of these types almost has a vernacular of its own.

TRADS	MODS
Let's get it blocked	Let's get analysed
Fix inflexions and "readings"	Play for sense and let inflexions take care of themselves
Block as soon as possible	Move freely for as long as possible
Play for laughs	Play for contact
Final decisions as soon as possible	Final decisions as late as possible and always open to reversal

TRADS	MODS
It was a bad house	It was a bad performance
I take orders	I give suggestions
Am I being masked?	Am I important at this moment in the play?
Can I be heard?	Are my intentions clear?
I'm getting nothing from my partner	I'm not getting what I expected, so I shall adjust
Just as we rehearsed it	As the immediacy of the performance dictates
Let's get on with it and stop intellectualizing	Let's apply what reason we have to the problems at hand
More feeling	More clarity of intention so as to produce more feeling
Hold that pause	Fill that pause
Everything's in the lines	Everything's in the sub-text
I'll play this role symbolically	I can't play concepts; only actions
I am the villain	I refuse to pass moral judgments on my character
My many years of professional experience convince me that ...	Nothing is ever the same

THEATRE OF CRUELTY

The first showing of the group's work unfortunately was titled "Theatre of Cruelty" and ran a scheduled five weeks at the LAMDA Theatre Club in London. It was never intended as a *show*, but merely a demonstration of work-in-progress, of interest, we assumed, to the profession. The press was not invited in the usual way, but letters were sent explaining that if they felt like coming along, they were welcome, but that we were not particularly desirous of reviews, as this wasn't strictly speaking a show. All of which was a kind of self-delusion that both Brook and I swallowed whole. Only after the event did the obvious truth of the situation strike us. Any presentation, call it what you will, that is done before an audience, invited or otherwise, becomes a show and is judged according to traditional criteria. This is not a harangue against the critics. On the whole, we got interesting, up-beat notices, but the point was that we weren't really intending a theatrical performance, and the overriding point was that it seemed impossible, in London, to present anything short of one.

The programme consisted of two short nonsense sketches by Paul Ableman, similar to our sound-exercises; a production of Artaud's three-minute *The Spurt of Blood* (played through first in sounds, then as Artaud wrote it); a dramatization, in movement only, of a short story by Alain Robbe-Grillet; two collages by Brook, one (*The Public Bath*) a splicing-together of newspaper accounts of the Kennedy funeral and the Christine Keeler testimony; the other (*The Guillotine*) made up from original sources; three scenes from Genet's *The Screens*; an anti-Marceauvian mime-sketch called *The Analysis*; a short play by John Arden, *Ars Longa, Vita Brevis* and the collage-*Hamlet*.

There were two sections in the evening which were deliberately marked out as "free". One, the improvisations, the forms of which changed every evening with the actors never being forewarned; and two, a section towards the close of the second half, into which we inserted whatever "specials" occurred to us. On the first night, Brook used this section to rehearse a scene from *Richard The Third*. Another night, the section was used for a spontaneous exchange between Brook and myself in which we questioned the audience's motives in coming to the theatre, and the whole point of what we were doing there. Early in the run, on the night John Arden was in the audience, without warning we asked him to come forward to justify his short play, and for the occasion we set against him one of the actors from *Ars Longa, Vita Brevis* who hated the play and what it was saying.

For the improvs, which I supervised from the stage, I tried to invent new and different challenges every night. On one occasion, we played the Changing Gears exercise entirely in sound; on another, entirely in musical phrases; on another, using only animal-noises. The audience was incorporated every evening and actors worked from suggestions thrown out to them from the floor. The random factors maintained a degree of freshness almost to the end of the run, but their main point was not simply to keep actors on their toes, but to break the hypnotic effect of continuous performance, and to unsettle the myth that grows up once a performance has begun a run. No two audiences saw the same show, and so no two people from different audiences could recount exactly the same memories. Towards this end, roles were swapped (frequently at the last moment); bits altered or dropped, and one piece (written by Paul Ableman) completely unstaged and unrehearsed, played out each evening as the spirit happened to move the actors. Some nights, this was disastrous; others, after it seemed that every possible interpretation had been tried, startlingly new moods would appear. The playing of this particular dialogue was greatly enhanced by the fact that the two players, who were sometimes required to play quite lyrically with one another, hated each other's guts. The tensions that charged, disfigured, and enlivened the piece prevented it from becoming dead material.

It is to the everlasting credit of Peter Hall and the Royal Shakespeare Company that it was understood from the start that this work required total subsidy. There was no question of making money or breaking even, for that matter, and it went without saying this was unrecoverable money (therefore, seats were deliberately cheap – five shillings each). There was no balking after the event, when accountants would solemnly point out £5000 had gone down the drain in a matter of twelve weeks. The drain, in this case, led to a very interesting cellar where certain rare wines were being cooled, and even if it should turn out they had all gone sour and had to be dumped, no one was going to burst a blood vessel or demand an official investigation.

PHASE TWO

After the Theatre of Cruelty showing, the plan was to begin work on Genet's *The Screens*. The group was enlarged to seventeen and training was re-started. The newcomers, who had seen the LAMDA programme and heard fanciful tales about the work, were wary and suspicious. The mother company was either distrustful or openly antagonistic towards the "mutation at Earl's Court", as one senior member described it. The original group of twelve, although still committed to the work, was beginning to eye the mother company covetously. They wondered what was going on at the Aldwych and where they would fit in. An inevitable concern and natural in the circumstances : twelve young actors working for peanuts with the prospect of graduation into a major London company. (An in-group definition of Theatre of Cruelty was twelve actors working for twelve pounds a week.) I mention this now, not to descend into theatre gossip, but to point out how even the best intentions can be subverted by an overpowering commercial atmosphere. Ostensibly, we had an experimental group concerning itself with craft-problems and difficult stylistic pursuits, but in fact, we had a group of talented, underpaid actors who were wondering how long they would have to work for subsistence wages. I don't want to exaggerate this under-current. It wasn't crippling or disastrous, but it did generate pre-occupations that affected the work. Training and rehearsals became, in some instances, miniature auditions for the better-paid work, and because the group, or some of them, were going to be assimilated into the larger company, it became impossible to build a healthily incestuous group-feeling; the kind of group-feeling that companies like Grotowski's in Poland, or the Beck's Living Theatre, build auto-matically because a shared attitude and mutual allegiance bind the company together. Good work can be done without such an adhesive; but not exceptional work; not enduring, un-self-consciously creative work.

The Screens:
The work on *The Screens* could be an essay in itself. The early exercises continued, and were gradually adapted to the specific needs of the play. The crucial production problem, apart from perfecting a style that would cope with such a monumental structure, was to communicate both the poetic and political tremors in the play with-out veering too far in one direction or the other. The Artaudian exercises had prepared us for Genet's metaphysics, and we now began to apply a Brechtian approach to get at the play's political bedrock, and also to define for ourselves precisely what each of those extravagant little scenes was about.

The early rehearsals were spent in reading, discussion, and trans-lation amendments. After rehearsing each scene, key characters were asked to tell the story of what had just happened : (1) as a factual news report; (2) as a policeman summing up before a magistrate; (3) as a fairy-tale ("once upon a time . . ."); (4) as a horror-story; (5) from the Marxist point of view; (6) from a Freudian

standpoint; (7) as it might be described by a highly poetic sensibility, etc.

Brechtian titles were employed as epigraphs for each scene.

SAÏD RELUCTANTLY GOES TO MEET HIS NEW WIFE
THE COLONISTS DISCUSS THEIR POSSESSIONS
SAÏD'S MOTHER INSISTS UPON BEING INCLUDED
AT A FUNERAL

Sometimes the work-sessions threw up more material than we knew
what to do with, and eventually the problem became one of discard-
ing highly interesting but irrelevant insights. More and more, we
concentrated on the text: its colouration, its timbre, its weight and
feel. As with Shakespeare, one began to test the truthfulness of
every moment in terms of the ring of the words in their context. We
found that every moment of naturalism, even the most obvious and
unquestionable, benefited by being knocked off balance; by being
winged by a metaphor, or studded with a stylization. *Ritualistic*
may be a critic's cliché when writing about Genet, but it becomes a
directorial Rosetta Stone in rehearsal. Even the crudest situation,
three soldiers farting a farewell to their dead Lieutenant (Scene 15),
becomes both more comic and more understandable by being acted
ceremoniously, instead of in a loose, naturalistic manner.

Like *The Blacks* or *The Balcony, The Screens* appears to be about
some great social topic (the Algerian War) but is essentially a
private fantasy couched in convenient social imagery. Saïd's salva-
tion through progressive degradation is portrayed with all the relent-
lessness of a thesis-playwright laboriously proving his point. As a
play, it proliferates incidents without opening up new ground, and
keeps winding back on itself like a badly wrapped package which
becomes fussy without becoming any firmer. Which is not to belittle
the genius of certain individual scenes; nor the breadth of the conception; nor the grandiose lunacy in the character of Saïd's mother;
nor the hypnotic other-worldliness of the scene where Madani is
transmuted into the Mouth of the murdered rebel-leader Si Slimane;
nor the easy, unpretentious shuttling between the worlds of the
rebellious living and the settled dead; nor the black, urinal comedy
between the Arab hooligans and the Algerian Cadi; nor the stunning
scene where Arab rebels paint their atrocities on to a series of ever-
multiplying screens. But on studying the entire play Brook felt, and

I concurred, that the first twelve scenes contained all the gnarled genius of the work, and the remaining two and a half hours held only endless out-riding variations.

One last observation on *The Screens*: in the work of no other writer is the external life of the play quite so essential. In the last weeks of rehearsal, *The Screens* looked murky and gauze-covered in spite of many weeks of trying to cut sense and meaning into the scenes. Then, using Genet's own colour suggestions, Sally Jacob's stark designs, and Brook's faultless eye for surface-effect, a great wave of colour was spread over the entire play. In the space of four hours (the hours during which costumes and design were added), the play was transformed into something bold, brazen, aptly rhetorical and hieratic, as if the arrival of objects and colour seemed to coincide with the arrival of Jean Genet. One part of me rebelled at what I took to be the spreading of dazzling camouflage, but another was entirely swept up by the camouflage itself. I am not simply describing the extra-dimensionalism dress rehearsals bring to a production. No amount of fancy surface can obliterate a faulty foundation, but in the case of *The Screens*, the costume and décor produced – in one day – two-thirds of the truth, only one-third of which had been evoked in six weeks of rehearsal.

Still, for me, *The Screens* was never an organic production, but a sub-structure and an overlay with a vital middle layer missing. The production made a kind of stark, physical sense in spite of, not because of, our work, and the intellectual uncertainty of cast and producers, the unresolved ambiguities in the text, left an inner fuzziness which a longer run would undoubtedly have revealed.

BROOK IN PERSPECTIVE: A DIGRESSION

Extended exposure to Brook enables one to balance him up. His greatest asset is that, because of personal charm and acknowledged past achievement, he inspires contributions from actors. They want to please him, and this desire makes them exert themselves more than is usual for actors. Brook is cunning in his use of praise or admonishment, cold-bloodedly applying one or the other depending on what effects he thinks he may achieve. He has a strong visual sense and an uncanny instinct for the structural needs of a production, but his approach to actors is too restrictedly intellectual and not always very practical. He knows how to describe the result he wants, but isn't always capable of producing it methodically. If an actor can transform Brook's verbal descriptions into acting-results, then the actor works well with him. If the actor either cannot understand what is being asked or cannot find the route to the result, Brook often cannot provide specific enough guidance. His approach to improvisation is external, seeing it mainly as acted-out stories that supplement a text rather than carefully devised provocations designed to induce missing qualities. Perhaps he distrusts the methodology of Method work because he has never grasped the technique of building beats and organizing systems to produce internal results, but because of this he is too often hoodwinked by flashy external choices.

Brook tends to work "off" rather than with people, and the preliminary spadework of aides and consultants helps him to eliminate possibilities in his own mind. In the midst of a stew of contradictory suggestions and ideas, he is able to bring to the boil a clearly defined line of his own, but he seems first to need the stew. He works best with outsize personalities like Scofield and Olivier because there it is simply a matter of adapting himself to highly creative instincts which already have a direction of their own, and Brook fully appreciates the value of letting talented actors have their own way. He could never build a characterization as Kazan does, nor could he ever exert that much personal influence on a role, but he is brilliant at using actors as objects. Although he has a firm intellectual grasp of a play's ideas, his natural instinct for violence and stark effects seduces him into irrelevant sensationalism, and often, as in his Paris production of *Serjeant Musgrave's Dance*, he is incapable of interpreting a play except in terms of his own personal obsessions.

His great attribute is a deep-seated distrust for any – even the best – of his rehearsal achievements. Being dogged by other and better ways to do a thing, he postpones final decisions until he is sure he has explored every possibility. His great liability is that he lacks the technique to explore acting possibilities, and too frequently, he settles for a *coup-de-théâtre* or a disarming stroke of cleverness. Although the *enfant-prodige* of the Forties is now a well-tucked-away image and the serious *metteur-en-scène* is more prominent, an impish cleverness remains Brook's constant enemy.

MARAT/SADE AND COMPLETION

When Peter Weiss's play *Marat/Sade* came along, it was the natural conclusion of the Group's work; a play which could not have been contemplated before the Group's existence and which now, after the work on Artaud and Genet, could not be ignored. The play even contained certain features from our first Theatre of Cruelty programme: Marat's bath-tub was mystically related to Christine Keeler's in *The Public Bath*, the guillotine imagery to Brook's collage-play. Weiss acknowledged Artaud as his mentor, Artaud had played Marat in a film for Abel Gance, sounds and "happenings" were embedded in the play in a way that had been integral to the Group's thinking from the start.

Although I cannot be absolutely objective about the *Marat/Sade*, I can be somewhat detached as I wasn't directly involved in its production. That it is a spectacular and breathtaking production – perhaps the boldest we are to see this half-century – seems to me unquestionable. It restores something riotous and vital to the theatre, a kind of stylized mania which is closer to the personality of Antonin Artaud than any other single thing. But just as the Group's work itself had been diluted by being a demonstration of techniques, so the production of the *Marat/Sade* appeared the ultimate application of a theory which had been hatched before the egg of the play ever arrived. It seemed to say: this kind of theatrical expression is soul-stirring and mind-widening – if only there was a play to accommodate it. Weiss's play, at base, is a rather old-fashioned and long-winded polemical tract. In the original Swinarski production which I saw at the Schiller-Theater before the London production, it was an indictment of revolutionary fascism that set out to make a Marxist point. One either took the play or left it alone, but it was what it was, and there was no question about its point of view. In the London production, its ambiance was neither political nor (despite polemical longueurs) philosophical, but exclusively theatrical. All the time it was saying: an Artaudian-inspired theatre, strong on imagery, disrespectful of plot and suspicious of theses, can resuscitate something in our jaded senses and overhaul our aesthetic appreciation. That I happen to agree with that implication does not blind me to the fact that this is not what the play is about. One tends to appreciate the work in somewhat the same way one admires the

resilience of a diving-board that allows a world-champion to perform a breathtaking triple somersault. Once the swimmer is in the
water, that diving-board looks mighty bare.

The *Marat/Sade* marked the dissolution of the Group, or rather
its assimilation into the larger company; the end for which it was
intended. One of Peter Hall's aims had been to use the work of the
Group as a kind of healthy anti-toxin which, after being injected
into the bloodstream of the mother company, would produce a
greater robustness. Actually, the arithmetic was all against that, as
there were seventeen in the Group and over a hundred in the
Company. I expected the LAMDA work would simply disappear.
As it turned out, it was the pivotal factor in the *Marat/Sade* rehearsals, and the key by which the overall company developed the style
of the new production. It was unfortunate that the LAMDA programme was called Theatre of Cruelty and that serious work should
have spawned yet another label for journalists to bandy about.
Where, on reflection, I have asked myself, where, in all of this,
was Artaud? It was never our intention to create an Artaudian
theatre – to do what, in fact, Artaud himself never did. But there
were so many provocative insights and tantalizing challenges in *The
Theatre and Its Double* not to take him up. What was Artaudian in
our work was the search for means, other than naturalistic-linguistic
means, of communicating experience and insights. Also, our attitude
to the classics – not as peerless masterworks, but simply as *material*
that could be reworked and rethought in very much the same way
Shakespeare reworked and rethought Kyd, Holinshed, Boccaccio,
and Marlowe. And what was characteristically Artaudian was the
shared distaste and impatience the Group's directors felt towards
prevailing theatre-trends; the well-upholstered, self-esteeming cul-
de-sac in which the contemporary theatre found itself.

The quest for Artaud, if it's lucky, will not simply discover
sounds, cries, groans, and gestures, but new areas that never even
occurred to Artaud. His value is that of the devastating sceptic whose
very posture and tone of voice questions the validity of highly
coveted achievements. How important is the accurate reproduction
of the trivia in our lives, asks Artaud? How significant is the arbitrary social thesis that elaborates a partial insight so that we are
persuaded this is the whole story? How valuable, asks Artaud, is a
theatre that elegantly, excitingly, and wittily reiterates the clichés

of our lives – compared to a theatre that suddenly opens up, like a mountain crevice, and sends down a lava that scours the lies, half-truths, and embedded deceptions of our civilization? "Metaphysical" has become a pretentious word with high-falutin' connotations, but if one defines it as a form of imagery through which we can rediscover the essential links between sky, rock, land, sea, gods, and men – that is a lesson worth learning, and one the theatre is not yet able to teach. The cruelty that Artaud referred to (this is a truism worth repeating) did not refer exclusively to torture, blood, violence, and plague – but to the cruellest of all practices: the exposure of mind, heart, and nerve-ends to the gruelling truths behind a social reality that deals in psychological crises when it wants to be *honest*, and political evils when it wants to be *responsible*, but rarely if ever confronts the existential horror behind all social and psychological façades. This is where Artaud becomes practical and level-headed, because he declares: if we want to have a theatre that isn't trivial or escapist, we have to find a new way of operating such a theatre: a new way of generating the actor into action, the playwright into meaning, and the public into consciousness. An exhortation couched in rhetoric isn't the same as a body of work and achievement, but at certain junctures in history – and I believe we're at one at this moment – it is the healthiest noise we can hear.

APPENDIX 3

Picasso's The Four Little Girls

LONDON PRODUCTION MEMOS

ITEM: After the event, as invariably happens when you fall into the grips of the media, I was asked: Why did you want to do *The Four Little Girls*? I forget the tenor of those replies but, as in all interviews, they were fashioned to suit the publication in question. The *Evening Standard*, a popular evening tabloid, is not interested in the aesthetic peregrinations that preceded a production, nor is *The Times* of London hell-bent on some gossip concerning Pablo Picasso. But whatever answers were given, it wasn't until a good deal later that I acknowledged the true answer to myself. I wanted to do it because it was impossible. Because after churning out, with varying degrees of success, an endless series of plays, revivals and other kinds of "feasible" projects, there is an exciting sense of all-or-nothing, a heady kind of moon-shot braggadocio, in turning to a task that everyone agrees cannot be done. Is this a legitimate pretext for a production? I remember when Chaliapin was going to play in a large opera house in Italy, they asked him in which opera he would like to appear: "The one which has always failed," he answered.

ITEM: Picasso certainly knew Artaud. They were both in Paris during the heyday of Surrealism. When Artaud was released from Rodez and a special benefit was arranged for him, much of the money raised for the event came from paintings contributed by Picasso. The feel of *The Four Little Girls* is clearly surrealistic. Almost automatic-writing; the writer flinging his mind against the walls of the unconscious to watch it rebound.

SECOND LITTLE GIRL: Let's act a play. Let's set the stage in front of the well and disguise the trees as waves. You, you'll be the ship-wreck, you the thunder and lightning and me the moon. You, you'll tell the waves to take off their nets and catch all the stars and the shells in their paws and throw them to us like pearl necklaces and march past on the blue table and the black chairs riding on cows and making faces. You, the smallest, you will offer them carrots, cabbages and tomatoes that we are going to gather on our knees singing, holding the veil by its four corners and you, during all this, you will light a great bonfire and throw on it all our dresses. We shall be naked and you, too, will undress at the same time and we shall go and hide under the table. But take great care not to burn yourself in the fire. Don't get too near with your pitchers full of wine. Some big rhubarb leaves that we shall plait around it will make the blackest of curtains for the tender mercies that the storm will let loose on us, when the waves come and seize us by the throat and wrap us up with their shrews. The greediest silence will fill its pitcher of fire and the broken wings of the horse that drags its guts in the ashes will open their grenades to a mirror filled with moons. When at a sign you will show you are going to bite, we shall all get up and we shall scratch our faces till they bleed. Then the honey from the well will disgorge all its bees and, pretending to be dead with fright, we shall laugh and sing our heads off together. The ship which will come on to the stage with all sails set, will be full of milk and blood and on fire, lit up by a thousand lanterns. [From Act I, as translated by Sir Roland Penrose. Calder & Boyars edition of *The Four Little Girls*.]

It is dreamlike, not in the style of Cocteau where every phantasmagoria has some verifiable classical root, but in the more freely associative, spook-ridden style of Max Ernst. Its stage directions are reminiscent of Artaud's for *Les Cenci*.

[*Enter an enormous winged white horse dragging its guts, surrounded by eagles: an owl is perched on its head; it stays for a short time in front of the little girl and disappears on the other side of the stage.*] – [Stage direction from Act IV.]

The same impossible happenings are described not as practical directions, but as a curious kind of poetic overlap to the spoken text. *Desire Caught by the Tail* was written during the Occupation in the Forties. It is charged with gloom, deprivation, austerity and foreboding. *The Four Little Girls* was written around 1948, when Picasso was living in Vallauris, very content, a family-man for the first time in his life, surrounded by rampaging neighbourhood children, entering into their games like the jubilating infant he wanted to be. That sense of ebullient childishness pervades the play. It celebrates what Picasso was fast losing and what had always meant most to him: the purity, the innocence, the unbounded and unpredictable creativity of childhood. The play, despite obvious parallels to his art, despite tell-tale signs from paintings from every period of his life, is not a painting in words, but a verbal attempt to engender tangible imagery. Words are used, as Artaud has exhorted Surrealists to use them, merely as part of the material of art, and by no means the main part.

ITEM: Meeting with Sir Roland Penrose, the translator and Picasso's official biographer. They were thrown together in Paris in the Thirties. A charming, exquisitely civilized man with a protective attitude towards El Diego, and a love he makes no bones about displaying. We sit in a grubby dishevelled upstairs office at The Open Space theatre; he, on a wobbly bed used as a prop – there being no seats in the room; I, leaning against a desk terribly conscious of our grubby surroundings. This man, who owns Picassos, who presumably lives well and eats well, is Chairman of the Institute of Con-

Three of the girls from the Open Space Theatre production, 1971, by
Marowitz of Picasso's *The Four Little Girls*
(*Photo Donald Cooper*)

Scenes from the Open Space Theatre production of Picasso's *The Four Little Girls* (*Photos Donald Cooper*)

The handkerchief scene in *An Othello*, produced by Marowitz at the Open
Space Theatre, 1972, with Judy Geeson as Desdemona, Rudolph Walker
as Othello and, *right*, Anton Phillips as Iago
(*Photo Donald Cooper*)

An Othello at the Open Space Theatre, with Anton Phillips, *left*, as Iago
and Rudolph Walker as Othello
(*Photo Donald Cooper*)

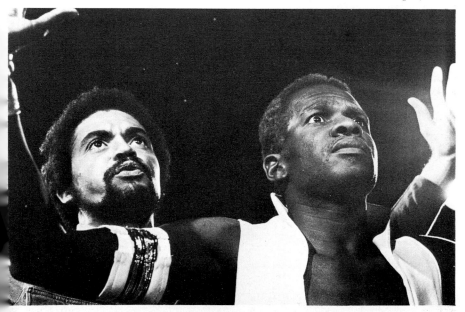

The murder of Desdemona in *An Othello*, with Anton Phillips, Rudolph Walker and Judy Geeson
(*Photo Donald Cooper*)

temporary Arts and a Knight of the realm, sitting on an unsteady prop-bed discussing aesthetics.

Anyone who wishes to form an idea of the main themes that have occupied the imagination of Picasso throughout his long and astonishingly productive life will realize that over and above the many problems of aesthetics, the invention of new styles such as Cubism, the intense pleasures of new and startling combinations of colour, the abstract enjoyment of geometric and organic form and the revelations, illusions and metamorphoses achieved in objects and sculptures that bring into question the nature of reality itself, none of these delights germane to the visual arts can diminish Picasso's passionate involvement with the human presence, not only in its appearance but more profoundly in its very nature and its daily behaviour. This being so it is not surprising to find a ceaseless eager inquiry into that most mysterious and intriguing period of life, childhood. But we learn from early drawings of urchins in the streets of Barcelona and the numerous mother and child paintings of the Blue period that the child to whom Picasso was most attracted was not a sanctified bambino nor a Little Lord Fauntleroy but rather the un-self-conscious product of human life, the child of the people, innocent and yet stuffed to bursting with the germs of all the vices and virtues of an adult. [Sir Ronald Penrose in the Preface to the Calder & Boyars edition of *The Four Little Girls.*]

I explain what I would like to do with the play. Penrose is unforthcoming. He asks questions politely. I answer them as thoroughly as I can. I am only riding hunches. I have no clear visions, only an impressionistic grasp of what I think can be made. He asks more questions. I have the slight feeling of being catechized. Still, I welcome the opportunity to formulate my own thoughts through questions that Penrose, as translator, can put better than anyone else.

In 1865, a rabbit-hole made it possible for the fair-haired Alice, a little English girl, to enter a country where wonders led to yet more wonders. In 1947–1948 the enchanted spot chosen by Picasso is a kitchen garden where four little girls, less elegantly groomed than their sister of Victorian times, frolic and evoke in games infused with freshness, wildness and often malice, life, love, death : a whole world of magic and of anguish to which adolescence opens the door. Songs, sayings, litanies, proverbs, nonsense, riddles are scattered throughout the play in which the author seems to use a language that is "holiday-making": heedless of the rules of logic and syntax, with images unfurling like Japanese flowers and, like the old woman who lived in a shoe, its poetry never ceases to breed as though it gave birth to itself in endless movement. [Michel Leiris in the Foreword to *The Four Little Girls*, Calder & Boyars edition.]

At the end of the session, Penrose rises suddenly from his unsteady perch, and gives the project his blessing. As we shake hands, his eyes are saying: "Please don't abuse my master." Mine are saying: "No guarantees. I'll do what I can."

In a language which is both innocent and sophisticated, using works and idioms that have a genuine ring of childish nonsense, the four little girls expound at length their fantasies, their dreams of ship-wrecks, their conversations with flowers, birds and animals, their mockery of adults, their visions of colour which invades itself and everything around, delicious combinations of coloured sweetmeats, wine and the merry-go-round at the fair. With innocent wisdom they speak in turn like a Greek chorus :
SECOND LITTLE GIRL : Only the eye of the bull that dies in the arena sees.
FIRST LITTLE GIRL : It sees itself.
FOURTH LITTLE GIRL : The deforming mirror sees.
SECOND LITTLE GIRL : Death, that clear water . . .
FIRST LITTLE GIRL : And very heavy.
Beneath the buffoonery and spontaneous joy of these four charming and precocious children runs the current of their main preoccupation with instinctive desires and fears: love, death and life. [From the Preface by Penrose.]

ITEM : A budget of £6000 is needed. Our total annual subsidy at The Open Space is only £5000 for some twenty productions. Letters are written; promotional material prepared. After six weeks of fierce fund-raising, we have only a pledge of about £500.

.   .   .   .   .

ITEM: Production scheduled to coincide with Picasso's ninetieth birthday, October 28th, 1971. Town councils, art-gallery owners, painters, collectors, and investors are besieged for funds. I am talked into meeting with Norman Granz at a posh London restaurant; he of the jazz concerts, is also, it appears, a collector of Picassos. Discussion is wrenched into politics; Black Panthers, revolution and American fascism. I am drawn out in order to support over-simplifications in crude political analyses. What has all this to do with Picasso? Agonizing communication barriers; dislike Granz and do not conceal it. Expensive lunch. A write off.

ITEM: Meeting with Victor Herbert, *avant-garde* promoter who financed *Desire Caught by the Tail* at St Tropez a few years before. Interested, wants a complete breakdown of precisely what the production will consist of. I say this is impossible as I do not know myself, and even if I did, would never dream of spelling it all out. No info, no cash. We don't buy pigs in a poke. Bye bye, Victor.

ITEM: Approaching casting period for *The Four Little Girls*; only £2000 raised. Impossible to reduce budget. Folly to proceed. I inform Penrose we must postpone until Christmas and use the extra time to raise the extra loot. General air of despondency; of having missed the crest of the wave.

ITEM: Money raised through excruciating fund-raising efforts too mind-blowing to describe. Penrose himself helps a great deal; resolved it shall happen. Casting now in earnest.

ITEM: Decision not to have a set designer but to bring in Carolee Schneemann, brilliant Happener, painter, film-maker; Penny Slinger, talented young English artist, Women's Libber and fantastic mask-maker; and Robin Don, rising young opera-designer, assistant to Ralph Koltai, and a practical Scot with an inclination towards tubing, metal, polythene and deft stylizations. Agreement that the play must take place on a fantasy terrain – like the world that Alice finds when she steps through the looking-glass.

SECOND LITTLE GIRL: You mustn't believe that the cat
has gone off behind the carrots to eat its eagle without fear or
remorse. The blue of its cry for pity, the mauve of its leaps and
the violent violets of its claws tearing Veronese-green rays from
the sulphur yellow of its rage, detached from the blood spurting
from the fountain full of vermilion, the ochre of the lilac wall
and the sharp cobalt fringes of its cries, the poor bird crouching
on the clogs of its feathers, acrobatic monkey, the flags smacking
their tongues on the steel and the knife already embedded, the
cat gathers together and lets go its shadows and its swords on each
floor, confused and confounded in the fall of verticals squashing
themselves drop by drop on the olive-green curtain. [From Act I.]

Agreement that "a setting" will not do; that the entire theatre,
from top to bottom, should be transformed into this fantasy terrain;
that the audience loll on grass, in the midst of the action. Agreement
that the overall concept will be a mixture of real and unreal
elements; that nowhere should there be a piece of verisimilitude
without, in some way, being knocked on the head. Hence, the grass
it to be pink, the trees, tubular, with knitting-wool foliage; the
bodies of the four little girls, clad in little girls' attire, but painted
different colours. Robin Don suggests an entrance way. A tiny doll's
house doorway beyond which looms the fantasy terrain. Each
member of the audience has the private moment of squeezing
through the doll-house door, past a cluster of concealing foliage,
emerging, like Alice, into an unexpected world of colour and magic.

FOURTH LITTLE GIRL: The blue, the blue, the azure, the
blue, the blue of the white, the blue of the yellow, the blue of the
red, the blue of lemon, the blue orange, the blue that oozes from
blue and the white blue, and the red blue and the blue of the
palms from the lemon blue of white doves, to the jasmin in the
fields of oats, in great almond emerald green songs. [From
Act I.]

Don's suggestion is the pivotal design choice for the production.

ITEM: Memo to casting director: "I want to see experienced
young actresses who look like pre-pubescent adolescents; no taller
than five foot one; pixie-faces and no tits. Must be able to handle

complicated poetic text." Reply from casting director : "You've got
to be kidding." Endless parade of long-in-the-tooth adolescents;
thirty if they are a day. Fat, blowsy dames who claim they possess
impish, childlike qualities; broads with Patton-tank boobs singing
"On the good ship Lollipop", as audition-pieces. Finally, after
screening some seventy girls, four sweet little things who can act,
none taller than five foot one, who actually do look like pre-
pubescent adolescents.

*[She arranges her doll, chained with garlands of flowers, in the
boat and ties it to the mast, lies on her back on the ground and
sucks and caresses the goat]* – [Stage direction from Act II.]

Only after rehearsals have begun am I told that all are over
twenty, and one as ancient as twenty-four. Note to myself : "They
didn't make 'em like that back on Second Avenue when I was
growing up."

ITEM :   Opening rehearsal remarks : "In every other play you've
ever done, you have asked, quite rightly, what is the meaning of this
speech? What is the motivation for this move, or that development?
Well, none of these questions will be allowed during rehearsals.
The play's meaning is something for us to invent – just as you sometimes invent your own meanings for abstract paintings. We will try
out arbitrary premises for each scene and specific sub-texts for each
line, and if they seem to work along with the text, we will incorporate them. If not, we will try other premises. So, no questions
about motivation; no questions concerning logic or overall meaning.
Clear?"

SECOND LITTLE GIRL :   Room full of farts . . .
THIRD LITTLE GIRL :   Old drain marmalade, bag of bed-
   bugs . . .
FOURTH LITTLE GIRL :   Sandwich gilded with shit . . .
THIRD LITTLE GIRL :   Black mouth of the sun full of
   cinders . . .
[From Act V.]

Four pretty little faces tentatively nod agreement wondering, as I myself am, does he know what he's talking about?

ITEM: Child's play. Children's games are calculated to create an ensemble feeling among children for the sake of some final, disruptive action, i.e. "Ring a Ring of Roses", "The Farmer's in the Dell", musical chairs, "Oranges and Lemons", the dressed-up primeval rite with its gaiety and togetherness leading to violence and demise. Having never played these games in my own childhood, rehearsals with my girls were truly educational. I decided to incorporate the ambivalence of the children's games into the show – first by playing them straight (with all the abandon of cavorting kids), and then in a sinister, menace-laden way, which would only underline transformations already contained in the games themselves. The same ambivalence was inserted right the way through the play with merriment segwaying into some diabolical antithesis of itself, brightfaced little sprites metamorphosing into bad seeds and imps-of-the-perverse. To celebrate childhood, it struck me, was to posit the very same contradictions of adolescence, maturity, or old age; of life, in fact. The intrusion of fantasy into reality; the conversion of light into shade; sense into nonsense; heaven into hell.

ITEM: Problem for the director. Suppress the organizing tendency of the conceptualizing mind. Forgo conscious structuring. Instincts, before they became known and understood, were impetuous little bursts that ran before experience. To reach them again, one must side-step the consciousness of anticipated experience. Work with the shut-attic part of the mind.

ITEM: Winged horses, battling insects and silver lakes, if approached literally, will destroy the texture of theatrical fantasy. I upset several designers by abandoning a winged prop-horse half-way towards completion; ditto two goats made of wire-mesh and fur. The horse is a tangible, man-made object that proclaims its components. It is as magicless as the cinema during intermission with all the lights on and the sales girls hawking ice-cream. Robin designs a skeletal horse painted with ultra-violet light which, in the dark, conveys the suggestion of a white-winged steed in flight. The goat is a lovely creation that would get admiring glances at an exhibition, but the actress who must play with it cannot hold it in her arms, and when she does, it looks like what it is, a prop. Search throughout toy shops for goats unearths a small-scale donkey which, when doctored and given plastic surgery, becomes an acceptable goat. The idea of our goat actually being a donkey, wearing the wire-mesh face of our abandoned goat, gives me a silent *frisson*. Picasso would have approved.

ITEM: What to do with that language? It isn't sense, it isn't poetry and yet, when played vigorously makes a kind of poetic-sense. But the girls are babbling it and treating it like the nonsense it appears to be. Breakdown of images. Knit together the parts of each speech – like individual beads on a chain. Keep thinking sub-text while propelling text and there is a flurry of sound-pictures like a Rorschach drawing on the move.

ITEM: Discovery! The text is not speech and does not yield to speech patterns. The speech is song, and the text must be sung, not melodically, but with a sense of chanting and incantation. One must musicalize the text, denaturalize it, without falling into the ever-open trap of pretentious poetry-music; the kind of sound we associate with mad Greenwich Village *soirées* in the Twenties, where gaunt ladies in floppy hats made arias out of Baudelaire. The girls are game. They sing; they dance; they turn the speeches into ballet; into animal sounds; into nineteenth-century melodrama. I grow fonder of them every day. I become aware of a kind of paternalistic attitude. I am Big Daddy. These are my young. I work the knickers off them and I know they bitch me during the coffee-breaks, but I acknowledge a palpable affection for them and, unless I delude myself, it is returned – minus the warmth I methodically freeze away worrying over our problem scenes. Ann Holloway, Susan Penhaligon, Mia Martin, Suzanne Williams. My very own Groucho, Chico, Harpo and Zeppo.

.   .   .   .   .

ITEM: The period comes when the show's tangible emblems and performer-made atmospheres must coalesce. The show is by Picasso; it is conceived in images and must be a feast for the eye.

[CHANGE OF SCENE: *The stage is painted white; back-cloth, wings, flies are covered with all the letters of the alphabet and large numbers painted in all colours. The floor is also painted in the same way. In the middle, a bed where the three little girls —* FIRST, SECOND *and* FOURTH *— are lying. Some enormous Winged Dogs wander round the stage by the bed.*] – [Stage direction from Act IV.]

[*The night falls. Some stars, the moon. All the stars. Some crickets. Some frogs. Some toads. Some cicadas. Some nighting-ales. Some fireflies. An intense perfume of jasmin fills the theatre and a dog is heard barking in the distance. Later, the whole garden lights up, each leaf is a candle-flame, each flower is a lamp of its own colour, each fruit is a torch and the ribbons of the branches of the trees are lights of separate flames. Shooting-stars fall like harpoons from the sky and plant their swords which open like roses and cups of fire.*] – [Stage direction from Act VI.]

For the first time in a production, I defer to the designers, and consciously subordinate the actors.

ITEM: The environment, conceived by Don, Slinger and Schnee-mann, is now taking shape. Two tons of foam rubber hug a series of scattered rostra, and a soft layer of raffia is sewn over the top. The interior of The Open Space looks like the outdoors of a children's fable. Graduating shades of pink roll into hillocks of purple, strewn with pink leaves (real leaves sprayed pink) and vegetables dyed all colours of the rainbow. A central well is also painted pink; beside it, a doll's house façade with painted windows. The girls are coloured yellow, orange, blue and mauve. When they cavort without clothes, their nudity is adorably unreal.

[THE LITTLE GIRLS *jump out of bed, naked. They lay out on the ground a large blue lake surrounded with flowers and bathe in it. From the middle of the lake the* THIRD LITTLE GIRL

emerges, also naked; her hair is covered with flowers and her
neck, wrists, ankles and waist are encircled with flowers; she
dances in the middle, holding the doll in her arms and the goat
on a lead. The Winged Dogs fly away. A CROWD *of photo-*
grapher-reporters enter and photograph scene from every side.] –
[Stage direction from Act IV.]

At one moment in the play, a lake made of melinex and polythene is rolled out as a naked little girl carrying sparklers strides
down it like a nymph rising from the sea. This is not exactly what
Picasso had in mind. I experience the insecurity every director feels
somewhere towards the end of a production. Is it really just a load
of rubbish? Who do I think I'm kidding? For the sake of harmony,
I divert the Medusa-like potency of my critical gaze.

ITEM: An environment inside a theatre is only a fancy name for
a stage setting – even if the setting happens to overflow into the
house. Since our object in the Picasso piece was tangibly to create a
fantastic outdoor terrain as it might be conceived by children, one
had, literally, to obliterate the theatre. Or so we thought. For after
removing all the seats and all the usual points of audience focus;
after building up rolling mounds of grass covered with pink leaves
and pink branches; after plunking down metallic trees threaded
with darning wool and ensconcing a stuffed-owl on one tree and a
twelve-foot snake on another, all we had really done was *theatri-
calize* an outdoor scene. The answer, clearly, was not to pretend to
a reality the convention excluded, but to use the convention as
artificially as possible to create the effect of a surrealistic terrain. The
secret of these transformations lies in texture. As the audience came
down the stairs of the theatre, they were confronted with a tiny little
door – like a doll's house entrance. When they bent down to step
through, they immediately confronted a bower threaded with
foliage. On the ground, they trampled dead leaves and multi-
coloured honeycombs. Nature, when you get down to basic defini-
tions, is *texturally* different from the man-made universe. The
quality of a leaf or a flower, an acorn or an apple is something that
industrial ingenuity can simulate but not create. The real "show"
in *The Four Little Girls* represented members of the audience experiencing the texture of an outdoor landscape *before* encountering

the characters – who capered through it. In one sense, the show was
a celebration of the environment – which is why the environment
had to be experienced first. Environmental theatre, which concentrates entirely on physical by-play between the audience, the space
and the actors, often forgets the essential factor that makes the
difference between a conventional or unconventional experience:
that the textural character of a space is what determines its "dramatic" effect on people. Arbitrarily intermingling actor and audience
only compresses traditional elements which, conventionally, are
separate, but the introduction of new textures – whether they be
grass or water or steel or rubber – and their engulfing effect on an
audience is what banishes the zombie-like demeanour of what we
tend to call "the spectator" because we traditionally expect him
simply to witness what we have prepared. A person physically involved in a new ambiance, but physically remote, might just as well
be sitting in a plush-chair facing a proscenium arch stage. The hang-
up of the environmentalists is that they believe that the tangible
creation of an environment *automatically* involves the audience,
which of course it doesn't. Environmental involvement depends not
on scenic factors, but on dramatic choices. No matter how elaborate
the scene into which you insert members of the public, unless a
dramatic imagination has acted upon the environment to further its
purpose in the overall scheme of things, you are simply cluttering
people with décor. Paradoxically, this produces the most conventional effect of all: a hyper-consciousness of the stage's artificial
materials; the kind of thing Belasco and Irving were doing a
hundred years ago.

ITEM: Throughout the play, the sounds have been either real
(woodland sounds, birds, dogs, etc.), or "distortions of real"
(electrical horse-whinnies, metallic cat-cries), but, apart from a faint
calliope at the start, there has been no music. Corny as music is, I
feel Picasso's last image, a white cube and an isolated glass of wine,
is essentially lyrical and requires something, just short of shmaltz,
to support it. I spend hours investigating my own collection – certain
it is violins I am looking for, and almost certain it is Vivaldi. The
discovery of the second movement of the Concerto in C is, for me, a
jubilant one. It is about as lyrical as anything can be and yet not

precious. The music accompanies the final movements of the play as the four little girls spread themselves on the centre of the terrain, slowly pull out four giant petals sewn into the ground, and wrap themselves up in them. As they settle back into the earth, an open-sided, white cube floats down and a pin-spot sends a "laser beam" on to a stark and shimmering glass of red wine. Kitsch, I mutter to myself at the dress-rehearsal; but really quite lovely.

Review of The Four Little Girls: *Positive (by CM)*

Mr Marowitz's production of Picasso's *The Four Little Girls* is wily enough to engage the play where it isn't. Realizing that he was working with a nonplay by a nonplaywright, there are none of those tedious questions of fidelity to script, or author's intentions. The play has been ferociously cut and liberally supplemented. The emphasis is on sight and sound rather than speech or character. The play proper is the instigating factor in the production, but by no means the most prominent element. Indeed, the production is an *amalgam of elements* suggested by the play, unrelated to the play, and in some cases, in contradistinction to the play. Like a Happening, it is easier to describe what occurs than what it is about. In a sense, it is *about* what *occurs*, and very little more need be said than that.

Review of The Four Little Girls : *Negative (by CM)*

Surrealism, apart from giving us Ernst and Breton, Artaud and Cocteau, has also bequeathed some of the most sterile intellectual exercises ever engineered by the unconscious mind of man. Picasso's *The Four Little Girls*, in this production by Charles Marowitz and collaborators, is a prime example of the vapid, aesthetic exercise which serves the self-indulgence of the author and the egoism of the director at the expense of an audience's well-being. Nonsense language and arbitrary actions commingle to produce a sequence of extravagant irrelevance, which makes one wonder why there ever was a Chekhov or a Shaw, a Brecht or a Shakespeare. The production takes refuge in the fashionable shelter of "meaninglessness for the sake of meaninglessness" and asks to be judged on the basis of specific effects, as if the notion of coherence and continuity was alien to dramatic art. The terrain, made of some kind of plastic grass and other artificial material, is highly uncomfortable and, as is to be expected at The Open Space, there are great doses of nudity served up in artistic tinsel to justify their salaciousness. Mr Picasso may be a very talented painter, but he's a rotten old playwright, and, as for Mr Marowitz, it would be interesting to see him take the liberties with a present, contemporary writer that he has taken with the absent, Spanish gentleman. I'd wager he'd get his teeth handed to him. And a jolly good thing too!

FIRST, SECOND AND FOURTH LITTLE GIRLS: Coming, coming, coming, coming. Let's go to war, war at home. Marsh-mallow angels, mice and rats, caramel night, jingle-bell morning. The bustle that goes on has made a mess in my sheets. Coming, coming, coming, coming. Life hides its vows to milk the cows. Life is fine, let's hide away from it. The calves are dead and have got wings. The wheel that turns undoes its dress and shows its breasts under the grass, the night hides its little fishes. The turtle-dove loves its turdle. Tell us, hollyhock, about this evening's sun-rise, tell us a story and make us laugh, take off your ball and chain, untie your rosaries, play your pistol for us on this bouquet of miserere moss-roses, how happy we are, happy to be together tomorrow, the day after tomorrow, today and yesterday.

  [*They turn around, jump and shout faster and faster, louder and louder and laughing fall to the ground on top of each other.*]

FOURTH LITTLE GIRL: We had a good giggle. I giggle. You giggle. She giggles. Happy happy happy happy, I am happy.

SECOND LITTLE GIRL: Happy.

FIRST LITTLE GIRL: I am happy, I am happy.

[*They start shouting.*]

Coming, coming, coming.

[*And innumerable birds are heard singing and a rain of eyes begins to fall on them . . .*] – [From Act I.]

APPENDIX 4

An Othello
Casebook

"The play was written within a period of about two and a half weeks. I felt very bucked by the fact that this was my first literary effort, literally dashed out within three weeks, and that it got a fairly interesting reception. The original idea was simply to edit Shakespeare's text, cut it about in a certain way, in order to bring out the black-white conflict theme, and I spent a lot of useless weeks fiddling around with the text trying to do that. I then wrote one small piece which I thought was necessary, and as time progressed, little by little, more stuff was added and more of the original was excised. So it was a very peculiar process in as much as one never really started out to write anything, one really did start out to edit and rearrange in order to get this particular story across through Shakespeare's play: but one found oneself out of necessity adding material, writing bits here, adding yet another scene, finding it necessary to put in a speech here, and so the end result was that two-thirds of the play turned out to be original writing and one-third Shakespeare.

"It was a great education, because I read Eldridge Cleaver and Malcolm X, James Baldwin and Stokely Carmichael – caught up with the last ten to fifteen years of black revolution in America. So there is not one original political idea in the play, they're derived, in fact, almost entirely from Malcolm X's ideas. The only original ideas in the play have to do with the divorce between the Shakespearian characters and their original context.

"I felt a great frustration always seeing *Othello* from a contemporary standpoint – that is to say, bringing to it contemporary anticipations – and never having those anticipations satisfied. The nature of the experiment was to see whether it was possible to take the anticipations that are engendered by Shakespeare's play and work them out in another fashion.

"Even Olivier's *Othello* unconsciously began to do this. Although the production-concept was entirely traditional, Olivier's own performance insinuated an alien idea which the play could not assimilate in spite of the actor's determination to foist it. Olivier cunningly reconstructed the behaviour of a black and grafted it on to the Moor. The fact that a Moor is not the same kind of social animal as a contemporary Negro had nothing to do with the case. Olivier was demonstrating his gifts of mimicry and we were going to get every physical detail of black behaviourism no matter what vital issues got lost in the process.

"The result was the kind of winning imitation we applaud in cabarets or music-halls, but in its very perfection it drew attention to fundamental contradictions. The play had no truck with attitudes towards contemporary negritude and the skills of imitation not only did not strengthen the fable but positively diverted us from its true centre. And yet, one could understand Olivier's desire to 'modernize'.

"It was my belief that there was no great relevance in reviving *Othello* today without accommodating the black revolutionary spirit irrationally lodged in an audience's expectations that made me want to tackle it; and by tackling it, I mean by-passing Shakespeare's original intentions and extracting only what I needed to achieve my own purposes.

"Malcolm X's distinction (see p. 169) between the House Negro and the Field Negro seemed to me to parallel that between the arm-chair liberal and the activist. And I think although one was dealing with the black political situation one was thinking very much of other things, if you like, which are closer to me than the black situation is. And all the way through the writing of the play, and the rehearsal of the play, there was this dogging fear of 'what right has this white New York Jewish intellectual to write about these things that don't directly pertain to him?' They do in the sense that I'm an American, but they don't in that I've not suffered the things that are dramatized in this play.

"*Othello* for me is a melodrama, but it happens to be a melodrama with a central black character, which creates impressions and ideas about black characters in today's world. I think the same thing is true about Shylock, and one thing that came out of my work on *Othello* was the realization that it was possible to do something along similar lines with the character of Shylock* – to release Shylock from that terrible prison that he's in, as a kind of comic character with tragic implications in an artistic context where he sticks out like a sore thumb. I could deal with *The Merchant*, you see, because I knew that if there were to be protests they would be from the Jewish Welfare Board and places like that – from my own people. I was a little more worried about *Othello* because I didn't want to have to deal with the Black Panthers.

"The critical reaction to *An Othello* generally was encouraging. I was peeved only by those people who, whenever one does Shakes-pearian experiments like this, invariably make bogus comparisons between the experiment and the original play, as if there's some kind of rivalry going on between me and Shakespeare. The reason that this version was evolved was simply because one couldn't say these things using the original play, and the constant reference back to the original, without accepting that this is an extrapolation from *Othello*, seems to me an indication of muggy-headedness on the part of the critics. Obviously no one is competing with Shakespeare. One is just taking certain segments, certain strands from the plays, and moving them in other directions. To try to analyse whether that is better than Shakespeare seems to me really irrelevant and very much off the point.

* This was achieved in the Open Space production of *Variations on The Merchant of Venice* which opened in May 1977.

"John Burgess, who compiled the production diary which appears below, served as my assistant for the production of *An Othello*. His own *Chicago Conspiracy* was seen at the Open Space in 1970, and we have collaborated on a translation of Arrabal's *And They Put Handcuffs on the Flowers*."

An Othello

by Charles Marowitz after Shakespeare

First performance at the Open Space Theatre, London on 8 June 1972

Desdemona	Judy Geeson
Othello	Rudolph Walker
Iago	Anton Phillips
Cassio	David Schofield
Brabantio	Edward Phillips
Duke	Malcolm Storry
Lodovico	Richard Monette
Direction	Charles Marowitz
Design	Robin Don
Lighting	Roger McDonald
Assistant Director	John Burgess
Stage Management	Harry Christopher
	Megan Doolittle
Production Assistant	Nora Peck

SYNOPSIS

Opening Tableau Lights up on Desdemona alone, tense and expectant. Great black hands come out of the darkness to embrace her. She yields to them and is spirited away amid noise and turmoil. *Scene 1* The abduction of Desdemona and preparations to meet the Turkish fleet. Act One of Shakespeare's play condensed into about seven minutes. Othello, black general in command of a white man's army, runs off with the daughter of one of the leading members of the Establishment. The Duke and Lodovico are reluctant to institute proceedings against him, since he is now urgently needed to repel the Turkish invasion. Iago is present on the sidelines throughout, a sardonic black jester. In place of Othello's big speech to the Senate, Iago has a long and bitter exposé of what it costs to be an Uncle Tom, the strains and compromises of making it in a white man's world.

Scene 2   The collage. Othello's memory of the storm at sea leads into the epileptic fit. The other characters get their hooks into him – literally – and pull him in all directions. He falls, and the events of the play, warped by paranoia, flash before his mind. He imagines a gloatingly adulterous Desdemona working in cahoots with the other whites to destroy him.

Scene 3   The interview between the Duke and Cassio. The first entirely contemporary scene in the play. Cassio appears as a young English subaltern, the Duke as a colonel from the American Deep South. The Duke gives Cassio a severe dressing-down for his drunkenness and then reveals that he is going to promote him in Othello's place. "We don't want a bloody coon general trottin' round these islands with a white pussy in tow and subvertin' the authority of our rule." Cassio is made to renounce his friendship with Othello, and then receives the Cyprus command in reward for his disloyalty.   .

Scene 4   Othello and Iago together, from the beginning of Shakespeare's Act IV, Scene 2. Egged on by Iago, Othello makes up his mind to kill Desdemona. He goes off, and Iago remarks how easily Othello's ambivalence towards her can be toppled over into murderous jealousy. "Ooh, ooh, he achin' to whip her ass so bad I think I's just wastin' my time plantin' little black seeds."

Scene 5   Second half of Shakespeare's Act IV, Scene 1. Othello gets the news that he has been recalled and that Cassio has been appointed in his place. Now that he's defeated the Turks, he's outlived his usefulness. He turns on Desdemona in a fury and slaps her face.

Scene 6   Desdemona's monologue, "Wouldn't you have if you'd had the chance?" justifying her marriage to Othello. Deep down every girl dreams of running off with a darkie but not everyone has the courage to make their dreams come true. Iago pours scorn on her view of the black man as a noble savage, possessed of natural rhythm – all the clichés of a muddle-headed romanticism.

Scene 7   From Shakespeare's Act IV, Scene 2. Othello and Desdemona confront each other. He is appalled by what he thinks of as her duplicity, she is baffled by his apparently unmotivated savagery.

Scene 8   Brabantio's monologue, "Would you like your daughter to marry one?" Brabantio appears here in his *alter ego* as a bigoted Jewish paterfamilias. His small-minded prejudice provides, besides comic relief, yet another variety of racial bigotry.

Scene 9   Othello launches into his Act IV soliloquy, "Had it pleas'd heaven To try me with affliction", with Iago in the background making derisive comments. Suddenly, with a scream of frustration, he drops right out of character and turns on his tormentor. He is no longer Othello the black general but Othello the black actor. Desdemona and Lodovico arrive, also as actors, and attempt to throw Iago the troublemaker out of the play. He ignores them, and concentrates his attention on Othello. He suggests to Othello that it's only right for him to kill Desdemona – after all it's no more than she deserves – but that he's quite wrong to turn the knife on himself – that's doing whitey's work for him. Desdemona and Lodovico retire discomfited. Iago confronts Othello. "It is the cause, it is the cause, my soul."

Scene 10   Lodovico, the Duke and Brabantio try to persuade Othello to ignore Iago's remarks and continue with his allotted role. Othello remains non-committal.

Scene 11   The last scene of Shakespeare's play, but here the black actor Othello has only half his mind on the job. He's busy working out the implications of what Iago has said. Desdemona the actress is thrown into a panic by his evident abstraction. He kills her (real or pretend?) and Iago appears to remind him that he need feel no guilt for what he has done, urging him once again to reject the course that the whites have mapped out for him. At the crucial moment Othello hesitates, knife in hand. The Duke holds him down while Lodovico cuts his throat. "And smote him thus." Iago drags out the body, while Desdemona rises to join the others. The victorious whites draw together in smiling complicity.

A DIARY OF THE PRODUCTION

The existence of the Open Space's newly formed permanent company makes casting at once easier and more difficult than it would otherwise be. A permanent nucleus of actors who are used to working together over a period of time has obvious advantages, but at the same time getting people in from outside – even when there's no one in the company who can play the parts – threatens the coherence of the group and is liable to cause bad blood. The point is underlined by news of William Gaskill's resignation from the Royal Court over what is essentially the same issue – a new plays policy versus the inevitable approximations of company casting.

At the outset everything is conditioned by the absence of a completed script, which makes detailed pre-planning impossible. Decisions on a number of important matters – design, costumes, props, and so on – which would normally be made before rehearsals begin are forced back into the rehearsal period itself, though Charles Marowitz has one or two preliminary discussions with Robin Don, who is to design the show. Casting is also affected. Charles is reluctant to make any definite offers until he knows what the final shape of the play will be, and several actors unwilling to wait any longer accept other commitments in the meantime.

The role of Iago is a particularly difficult one to cast, as it requires someone who can cope equally well with blank verse and Black Panther slang. Time and again we find people who are right for one but not the other. Our search isn't made any easier by *The Stage*, which refuses to carry our ad. for a black Iago: apparently it's in contravention of the Race Relations Act. There is even a moment when Charles, in despair, toys with the idea of shelving the whole project – which would mean for the second year running dodging our commitment to the Wiesbaden Festival, which has commissioned the work. The arrival of Anton Phillips saves the day. Born in England, he has lived for several years in the United States: the dual nature of the role holds no terrors for him. He is offered the part a week before rehearsals are due to begin.

Monday 1 May
Read through at 11.00 p.m. Rehearsals had been scheduled to start this morning but this is the first time we're able to get everyone together, and the cast collect their scripts as they arrive. We are all seeing them for the first time, and the three actors from the permanent company still don't know what parts they're supposed to be playing.

Charles reads the passage from Malcolm X about the House Negro and the Field Negro.

Back in slavery days there was what they called the House Negro and the Field Negro. The House Negroes lived in the house with master, they dressed pretty good, they ate good because they ate his food – what he left.

They loved the master; and they loved the master more than the master loved himself. They would give their life to save the master's house – quicker than the master would. If the master said, "We got a good house here," the Negro would say, "Yeah, we got a good house here." Whenever the master said "we", he said "we". That's how you can tell a House Negro.

He identified himself with his master more than the master himself. And if you came to the House Negro and said, "Let's run away, let's escape, let's separate," the House Negro would look at you and say, "Man you crazy. What you mean, separate? Where is there a better house than this? Where can I eat better food than this? Where can I wear better clothes than this?" That was a House Negro. In those days he was called a "house nigger" and that's what we call them today because we still got some house niggers running around here.

This modern House Negro loves his master. He wants to live near him. He'll pay three times as much as the house is worth just to live near his master and then brag about, "I'm the only Negro out here, I'm the only one on my job, I'm the only one in this school."

On that same plantation, there was the Field Negro. The Field Negroes – those were the masses. There were always more Negroes in the field than there were Negroes in the house. The Negro in the field caught hell. He ate left-overs. In the house they ate high on the hog. The Negro in the field didn't get anything but what was left of the insides of the hog. They call it "chitlins" nowadays. In those days they called them what they were – guts. That's what you are – gut-eaters. And some of you are still gut-eaters.

The Field Negro was beaten from morning to night; he lived in a shack, in a hut; he wore old, cast-off clothes. He hated his master. He was intelligent. That House Negro loved his master, but the Field Negro – remember, they were the majority, he hated the master. When the house caught on fire, he didn't try to put it out; that Field Negro prayed for a wind, for a breeze. When the master got sick, the Field Negro prayed that he'd die. If someone came to the Field Negro and said, "Let's separate, let's run," he

*didn't say "Where are you going?" He'd say, "Any place is better
than here." You've got Field Negroes in America today. I'm a
Field Negro. The masses are the Field Negroes.*

*Just as the slavemaster of that day used Tom, the House Negro,
to keep the field Negroes (i.e. Revolutionary Negroes) in check,
the same old slavemaster today has Negroes who are nothing but
Uncle Toms. To keep you and me in check, to keep us under
control, keep us passive and peaceful and non-violent. That's
Tom making you non-violent. It's like when you go to the dentist
and the man's going to take out your tooth. You're going to
fight him when he starts pulling. So he squirts some stuff called
Novocaine in your jaw, and you suffer – peacefully. Blood running down your jaw and you don't know what's happening.
Because someone has taught you to suffer – peacefully.*

*The slavemaster took Tom and dressed him well, fed him well
and even gave him a little education – a LITTLE education; gave
him a long coat and a top hat and made all the other slaves look
up to him. Then they used Tom to control them.*

*The same strategy that was used in those days is used today by
the same white man. He takes a Negro, a so-called Negro, and
makes him a celebrity. And then he becomes a spokesman for
Negroes – and a Negro leader.*

After the read-through Charles asks for comments or reactions –
anything which will help him gauge the effectiveness of the script
as it now stands. Silence. One or two of the company pick out points
relating to their parts (the characters' lack of internal consistency is
an obvious source of difficulty), but no one offers any general
criticism. Charles says that listening it's become apparent that several
bridge passages are needed to knit it all together, and that the script
is generally too long. One and a quarter hours is, he feels, the
optimal running time. The reading lasted an hour and a half and
there's another scene still to come (Scene 9).

Tuesday 2 May
Have the morning off to recover from last night's session. No respite,
however, for the actors in the permanent company – David,
Malcolm and Richard. They have an opening today, a lunchtime

production of Howard Brenton's new play *How Beautiful With Badges*, and are called for a dress-rehearsal at 11.0 a.m.

Reading the play in detail at 3.0 p.m. In the first scene, Charles steers Brabantio(Edward Phillips) away from indulging his private grief over the loss of his daughter. What he wants to stress here is Brabantio's race hatred of Othello – the social rather than the political content of the scene. In Scene 4 Charles stops the actors and warns them that it's coming out too conventional. The key to Iago's behaviour here is his exaggerated puritanism. It's this apparent prudishness that enables him to lead and bend Othello to his will.

Spend most time, however, on Scene 2, the collage. Out of a cast of seven, four have already worked with Charles on his *Hamlet*. The other three, Iago, Othello and Desdemona, are new to collage technique and are evidently a bit puzzled by the rapid switches of mood and characterization that it requires. One minute Charles is telling Judy Geeson (Desdemona) to play like something out of the *Great Waltz*, the next like Ingrid Pitt in a Hammer horror movie.

Wednesday 3 May
Charles brings in copies of Scene 9 that he's spent the morning finishing. Judy phones in to say she has food poisoning and can't make rehearsal, so we have to work on those parts of the play that don't involve Desdemona.

Interview between Duke and Cassio. Charles tells Malcolm Storry (Duke) not to use too much force. "Cassio should be terrified but you should not be terrifying. You have the power of life and death over him and he knows it. Real homey, real crackerbarrel. You don't need to assert yourself." Block the scene after reading it – Charles rather forcing the pace. Rehearsals have started a week later than planned because the script wasn't ready and the opening night in Wiesbaden is only three weeks away.

Going on to Scene 4. What Charles wants to get across here is that Iago and Othello essentially share the same world. Whatever their differences they have a deep instinctual sympathy with each other that they do not share with any of the whites in the play. Rudi breaks off to ask how stiff and military he should make Othello. Charles says this is chiefly important in the early scenes where we see Othello in his social role as the white man's general but it doesn't matter so much here.

MEMO FROM MAROWITZ FOR OTHELLO
FALSE HYPOTHESES RE OTHELLO
What is this black general doing at the head of a white army fighting Turks who, if not actually black, are certainly closer to his own race than his Venetian masters? Why is he the only black in the play? Are we to assume he is some kind of splendid oddity in an otherwise white society? That no racial tension exists in the state in spite of miscegenation, senatorial bigotry and wars waged against non-whites? These are not historically based speculations but a series of false hypotheses created by the desire to stretch old material into new shapes for no other reason than to see them hang differently. Pure perversion.

FICTITIOUS ANSWERS TO FALSELY HYPOTHETICAL
QUESTION
Othello is an awe-inspiring Uncle Tom. Only a toadie and a relentless brown-nose would have worked his way up the ranks to the position of General. Only a racial traitor would have accepted the ideals Othello has had to support to reach his exalted position.

What is a black celebrity in a white world? He is a tool of white society to placate the hostilities of the black masses. His success shines like a clear white light in an otherwise grim and black world. The appropriation of one black man into the privileged suburbs of white society dismantles the revolutionary impetus of a thousand black renegades. The privileged black — the bourgeois black — is the single greatest barrier to reform for, so long as his security is at stake, he will rationalize the reactionary instinct which parades itself as "moderation" or "gradualism". Othello in a white context is noble, courageous, forthright and commendable. But place one other black into that context and his credibility is immediately undermined. Fill it with thousands of members of an underprivileged black society and his position is morally untenable. CM.

Production meeting at 5.30 p.m. Robin Don, our designer, brings in his costume sketches and model. He looks exhausted, having seen up till 5 a.m. that morning trying to get the Duke's costume right. The problem is to find something that will look equally natural both in the Shakespeare and in the contemporary scenes. Worried that the well-styled anonymity of Robin's designs may be too reminiscent of science fiction, and suggest that a modified version of battle fatigues might do the trick, but Charles, not wishing to arouse associations with the Vietnam war, favours something less specific.

The production will in fact have two sets. One in Wiesbaden which the Germans are going to make for us, and another for the run at the Open Space. Everything needed for this will need to be planned in great detail before we leave so that it can be built while the company are abroad. After the performances in Wiesbaden on 26 and 27 May we have another date booked in Stuttgart for 3 June. Wonder if Wiesbaden will let us borrow their set for this extra performance, or whether everything will have to be shipped out from England.

The set is a cage with ropes for bars, which will surround the actors on all four sides. Discuss how to get the furniture on and off – Desdemona's bed constitutes a particular problem. In Wiesbaden Charles wants a huge handkerchief 18-foot square to float gently down from the flies. How will this work at the Open Space where the ceiling is only 11 feet above the stage? What thickness should the ropes be? Charles favours two-inch diameter for Wiesbaden. It's an enormous theatre and he's afraid that anything thinner will just disappear. Robin says that two-inch ropes will be fantastically heavy and also very expensive. Decide to go down to the rope shop and look at samples.

The discussion continues during supper and at 7.0 p.m. we resume with as much of Scene 1 as is possible without Desdemona. Charles points out that Brabantio has no doubt that Desdemona will obey him because never in his life has it occurred to him that she might have desires of her own. When she announces her determination to stay with Othello he is forced to look at her with new eyes. She's no longer just an object but a person in her own right and he doesn't like it. Finish by blocking Scene 10.

Thursday 4 May
Judy is still ill. In the morning the interview between the Duke and Cassio again. Malcolm is asked to overlay his speech about clouds

and their essential whiteness with a lyrical, creamy tone. It makes much more sense like this – not a reasoned argument, but a profession of faith, and suggests the deeply habitual nature of the Duke's racism.

Charles goes to the dentist over lunch and we start the afternoon without him reading over the collage. When he gets back, block Scene 1. The problem is to establish a solid, conventional *Othello* on which Iago can comment. At first the extreme compression of the writing tempts the actors into comedy. Cassio, who is here incorporating all the messengers as well, is running in and out of doors as if he were playing a Feydeau farce. The difficulty is to combine this accelerated pace with the proper Shakespearian weight, otherwise the contrast between the formality of the sixteenth-century verse and Iago's contemporary slang goes for nothing. Charles: "If we're going to hear the thud of Shakespearian verse anywhere in the play it should be here." It's uncertain to what extent this will allow for any original interpretation of the Shakespearian scenes. Charles decides they should be "square but not dull". Rudi is asked to play the line, "Her father loved me, oft invited me", reproachfully to Brabantio. It becomes clear that Othello was a welcome enough visitor – until he broke the rules by running off with the Senator's daughter.

Finish the day with Scene 10. Charles: "Although it's an important scene the effect of it isn't very explicit – which is as it should be. It should create a sense of mystery in the audience. They should feel that there's something important at stake, yet not quite be able to put their finger on it."

Becoming apparent that one of the chief difficulties on this production is going to be simply getting people together to rehearse. Rudi spends his mornings down at Thames Television finishing work on the series *Love Thy Neighbour*, while the three actors from the Open Space company are playing at lunchtime in the Howard Brenton play and at night in the collage – *Hamlet*. This means that they're only available between three and six in the afternoon, or for a couple of hours in the morning – which without an Othello is of limited usefulness. Five scenes – nearly half the play – are still untouched except for a preliminary reading.

Robin comes in to discuss Brabantio's costume, which is proving particularly awkward. All the other characters wear uniforms of one

sort or another and it's a comparatively easy matter to stylize them
till they provide the required degree of ambiguity. Brabantio is the
only civilian in the play and it's difficult to find something that
doesn't look either too trendy or too fantastic.

Friday 5 May
Brabantio's monologue. Wonder whether to make him an American
or an English Jew. Decide to go for the former. As more details are
added the speech begins to sound a little too deliberate. Charles
reminds the actor that volatility is the essential thing to go for
here.

Judy is back with us today so we start work on the collage. Charles
asks everyone to lay on the colours in broad bold strokes. The scene
opens with a twelve-line exchange between Othello and Desdemona,
taken from Shakespeare's Act II Scene 1. The whole of their loving
relationship has to be compressed into this short space. There is no
time for a naturalistic build-up. The actors have to hit the emotion
true and clean and first time off and then after twelve lines erase it
completely with something else.

Blocking is extremely complicated and takes to the end of the
day. Cassio is forever fixed in Othello's memory as he kneels before
Desdemona asking her to intercede for him. Charles asks him to
turn and bury his head between Desdemona's thighs: the gesture
of respect is suddenly transformed into oral sex. It's a very effective
trick and takes us all by surprise. Charles looks pleased.

The gang-bang sequence, where Othello imagines Desdemona
whored by "the general camp, pioneers and all", takes quite a bit of
working out. Charles asks Cassio, the Duke and Lodovico to lie
chest uppermost, supporting themselves on their outstretched arms
and heels. Desdemona then lies on top of them one by one as they
pump their hips up and down. The business of clambering from
one to the other proves too cumbersome however. Richard Monette
suggests a neater orgy that was used in *Oh! Calcutta!*, which though
still fairly gymnastic is a good deal easier to execute, and is adopted
for the time being.

Brabantio's costume again. At 6.0 p.m. Robin has come up with
a sort of suit and cloak combination but it's still not right. The shirt,
the tie and the cut of the collar make it too unequivocally modern.
Trouble too with the handkerchief. When is a hankie not a hankie?

Answer: when it's blown up to 18-foot square, in which case it becomes a tablecloth.

Saturday 6 May
Start by reading Scene 9, then stagger through the collage a couple of times. Charles asks the actors to learn the scene by Monday so that they can have total freedom of movement – at the moment it's looking a bit dull and static. Experiment with sounds for the gang-bang. Charles wants something that suggests "not just screwing, but total, gross infidelity". Decide on a sucking sound overlaid with heavy breathing.

Charles passes the week's work under review. There are three groups of characters in the play – Iago, the agitator; Shakespeare's characters, Othello, Desdemona and Cassio; and the authority trio, Lodovico, Brabantio and the Duke. These last are meant to be the Establishment figures of the play and of the society. They should really be older men, and the actors' relative youth constitutes a problem. The Duke and Lodovico are emerging as too lightweight, in a way that detracts from the impact of the piece. Charles suggests that they go for something suggestive not so much of age as of maturity. He feels that Cassio is at the moment a character made up of individual beats but without a true centre to him. Who is he? What is his relationship to Othello? What kind of a friend is he? Because these questions haven't been answered, Cassio is in danger of becoming just an empty shell.

Final version of Brabantio's costume decided on – with collar instead of ruff.

Sunday 7 May
Charles works at home with Anton on Iago's long speeches.

Monday 8 May
Run scenes already blocked. The actors are off the book for the first time with all the attendant uncertainties. The Duke and Lodovico are directed to play the section of Scene 1, "There is no composition in these news that gives them credit", at a high pitch of hysteric fear as if they were nervous schoolgirls. Charles then asks them to go back over the scene and cover it all up. After lunch, block the remainder of the play, including the opening section.

Struck by how little the actors are contributing to the shape of the production. It's partly, I suspect, that they rather stand in awe of Charles as author-cum-director: and partly that the play itself gives them comparatively little scope for invention. Each scene is constructed to make one specific point and the main function of rehearsals is to see that each point gets made as clearly as possible. Everything else is stripped away. The effect of this is to throw more weight on the director's contribution since he is the sole arbiter of what is or is not relevant, and to discourage any independent invention as being superfluous.

MEMO FROM MAROWITZ FOR THE COMPANY
LEVELS OF ACTION FOR CONSIDERATION

1   Actors playing in Shakespeare's Othello *are confronted with a threat when a maverick appears in their midst. All are concerned, but the greatest threat is to the actor playing Othello, for the black actor usurping the role of Iago gradually makes him realize that his performance is an integral political factor in a so-called classic which has been playing in the same way for almost four hundred years.*

2   The characters in Shakespeare's play gradually become detached from their context. Characters like Iago, Desdemona and Othello, apart from being dramatis personae *in Shakespeare's work, are also characters in the received world of literature. In a sense, they are* alienated *by tradition for, so powerfully have they been delineated by the past, they almost exist as characters (personages) in their own right. On this level, these "personages" comment upon certain implications in the play which gave them birth — like children who have grown up and are able to see their parents and place of origin with a new objectivity.*

3   Othello operates in an imposed political context which alters his character and compels him to justify his action in terms of the black power struggle. Iago is the instigator of these feelings.

All of these levels intermingle. They should not be clarified or separated. They should intertwine. The play proper — that is, some kind of straight rendition of Shakespeare's play Othello — *is the necessary foundation for all of these accretions. Some fundamental part of the performance must be a conventional rendition of Shakespeare's work – not as parody or satire, but as it might be in a sober, respectable classical production.* CM

Tuesday 9 May

Interview between the Duke and Cassio. Charles asks the actors to play it reversing the power situation, with Cassio very confident and the Duke completely unsure of his authority. Sit round and discuss the results of this. The point of the scene is that Cassio does not exist for the Duke as a human being. The moment when, as in this exercise, the Duke begins to take account of Cassio's feelings, he can no longer operate. What the Duke is doing is simply changing Cassio's usage, "like taking a broom and making it into a toilet plunger".

CHARLES: What is the Duke's action in this scene?

MALCOLM: To get Cassio to take Othello's place.

CHARLES: That's the *story* of the scene but not what the Duke wants in a dynamic relationship with Cassio – which is to change him to fit in with your conception of what you want.

It's decided that the Duke has three actions in the scene which can be expressed as follows:

1. I demand you be what I want you to be.
2. I demand you think as I do.
3. You *will* be what I want you to be

Cassio also has three actions:

1. I want to stay in the service at any price.
2. I want to understand.
3. I want things to be simple.

The actors are asked to now play out the scene using only the three lines they've chosen – or components of them. Then they are allowed only one word each – "Be" for the Duke and "Service" for Cassio – with which to express their intentions. Finally we return to the scene as written, but this time, although the Duke is using his full text, Cassio can only use his feet to reply with.

Scene 7 in the afternoon. Desdemona's action here: "I want to discover what's happening to you." Given that Othello is convinced of Desdemona's guilt why does he never confront her with it? Charles says that in this scene Othello half believes that Desdemona is a devil. He asks Judy to do the scene from this standpoint, while Othello carries on as normal. Desdemona is now transformed into a Fury, taunting Othello, pinching and teasing him. Charles points out that even when the scene is done straight that is what Othello should be seeing in his mind's eye. Finish the day with a stagger-through of Scenes 4, 5, 6, 7 and 9.

Wednesday 10 May

Improvisations. Desdemona and Brabantio play out a domestic scene together in which he is an American senator worried by his popularity ratings and what the neighbours will think, and she breaks the news to him that she's going to marry a Negro. The defeated father gasps, "Wait till your mother hears of this." Cassio is put on trial for drunkenness by the other actors. They prepare to acquit him if he can manage somehow to shift the blame on to Othello. Desdemona is the ringleader here. Another trial for Iago, more hostile this time. If he knew Cassio couldn't hold his liquor, why egg him on? Break for lunch. Iago saved by the bell.

The idea of these improvisations is to force the actors to find justifications, at gun point as it were, for the way their characters behave. Choices made under the pressure of interrogation can subsequently be tested to see if they fit.

Work on the collage in the afternoon. Experiment with the ropes for the storm and epileptic fit. The actors come on in blackout, fit the ropes on to Othello (five in all – one round his waist, one on each forearm, and one in each hand), and wind the slack round their own waists. When the lights come up on the storm scene, the Duke, Cassio, Lodovico and Brabantio are discovered in a tight group round Othello with not a rope in sight. At the point of transition into the epileptic fit each character spins outwards to the full extent of his rope; Othello in the centre is pulled in five different directions at once. A substitute handkerchief 12-feet square has also arrived, and we try out the various possibilities for Desdemona's death. These two images are part of Charles's initial concept of the scene. We're now seeing them fleshed out for the first time. Re-do some of the previous blocking to give the scene more depth. At the moment people are tending to end up in a straight line downstage.

Thursday 11 May

Charles spends the morning at L. W. Hunt's, looking over voodoo drums. Work on Scene 3, ploughing back the results of Tuesday's session. Problem with the clichés in Scene 10. The actors are trying to mine them for a meaning and significance that they do not possess, which gives the scene an unnaturally ponderous air. After lunch start blocking the last scene. It's uphill work. The essential action happens in the pauses, which gives the actors very little to latch on to. Charles, ruefully: "It's probably impossible, what we're trying to do here." When Iago comes on after Desdemona's death he is told to be as still as possible and not subvert the mood with any un-necessary movement. "You're playing what's going on in his head." Block Brabantio's monologue.

Friday 12 May
Having second thoughts about the set. Wouldn't *chains* do better than ropes for the bars of the cage? Ring Wiesbaden to find out if it's not too late to change our mind.

Work on Iago's long speeches, and go over Scene 10 carefully grading the build from fulsomeness to open anger. Start the after-noon with the last scene again. Beginning to get the hang of it now, though the temptation to play the scene for its full Shakespearian value is still proving hard to resist. Cassio and Lodovico are having difficulty getting their speeches after Othello's death mechanical enough. The physical exhilaration of the murder is being carried over into the lines.

Charles asks Rudi to set aside the text for the time being, and play out his unspoken thoughts. By the time we leave the scene it's begin-ning to take on the right eerie, disassociated quality – everyone saying one thing and meaning another. The collage however re-mains obstinately stagebound. Change the orgy again. Desdemona is asked to lie sideways across the bodies of the three men. Charles prefers this as being less explicit.

We're working this afternoon in the gymnasium of the YWCA. Half an hour before we finish, the local squash club come in and disrupt the rehearsal. Heated argument ensues, which results in the unhappy sportsmen being thrown out by the caretaker. We're doing Scene 9 at the time, in which the other actors get together to throw Iago out of the play. The work profits greatly from the interruption, the actors channelling their resentment into the scene so that, for the first time, it hits the right note of embarrassed, self-righteous anger.

Suspect the whole incident of having been engineered for this purpose.

Saturday 13 May
Summing up the week's work. Charles feels generally that the production is in poor shape and will need a great deal of hard work over the next ten days if it's to be at all presentable by the Wiesbaden opening. First run-through. Suspect this is Charles the author rather than Charles the director, who usually disdains straight run-throughs as time consuming and irrelevant, preferring to keep working on scenes in detail right up to the last minute, and if he runs at all is always sure to introduce some modification – that everyone should sing their lines, or dance them, or whisper them, or even replace the dialogue with pure sound. The run lasts two hours and feels like three. Charles and I agree to cut the play independently over the weekend and compare notes. Wonder if Charles will be able to be sufficiently ruthless.

Finish the day with Scene 7. Judy is told to stand up to Othello here. "One wants to get the feeling that the occasional tiff is part of their relationship and that Desdemona is capable of giving as good as she gets."

Sunday 14 May
Cut the play heavily to compensate for any reluctance on Charles's part, and decide privately that Scenes 9 and 10 need rewriting. Wonder whether to voice these doubts.

Monday 15 May
Charles spends half the morning at Theatre Projects supervising the recording of the sound effects for the storm. Talk through the last scene. Actors still very unclear. Talk about what they're supposed to be doing here. Point out that the play falls into two halves, the first half being about Othello the character, the second about Othello the actor. The piece is structured more like a revue than a play and anyone looking for a consistently developing character is going to get very confused indeed.

Seem to have made the wrong decision over cuts. Charles obviously feels that my suggestions are irresponsibly sweeping and rejects them out of hand. Figure I'd best not mention rewrites under the circumstances.

Wardrobe mistress comes in with a preliminary version of Judy's dress. Decide that the material chosen doesn't look right and it will have to be done again.

Going on to Scene 3 after lunch. Malcolm is now taking too long to effect his mood changes here and inserting long sinister pauses. Tighten it all up. The point of the scene is lost unless the switches between lyricism and threats are perfectly clear cut.

Back to the collage. The actors are now safe on lines and Charles pushes them harder for speed and attack, saying it should in the end go at roughly twice its present speed. Problem with ropes. How long will it take to wind into them – not forgetting that it all has to be done in the dark? If it proves too complicated they may have to be cut. Restage the orgy again. This time Desdemona is underneath and the men on top. Run the scene again after tea, trying to get the intentions absolutely clear. It's still not working properly and Charles wants to see if there isn't some basic flaw in the construction that's at fault. Finish the day with Scene 11. Charles provides a minutely novelistic account of the characters' feelings.

Richard Monette: "Charles certainly directs more than anyone else I've ever worked with."

Tuesday 16 May
Wiesbaden ring to say that they've already bought the ropes and it's too late to change now. One can't blame them. Estimated cost of the ropes is £800.

Scene 5. Othello's action here: "I don't want Desdemona around while I'm occupied with official business – especially when that business involves me losing my job." At the moment Othello is playing primarily to Desdemona and only secondarily to Lodovico whereas it should be the other way round. Lodovico is the real centre of the scene.

Going on to Scene 8. Eddie Phillips is asked to take two very different characters – a very proper upper-middle-class Englishman and a grotesque Fagin-like Jew – and play his monologue switching rapidly between them.

Scene 7. On the line, "O thou weed who art so lovely fair and smell'st so sweet That the senses ache at thee", Othello should be saying "Yes" with his voice but "No" with his body. The tension here is being blurred by a too general lyricism. At the end of the scene Desdemona should not break until Othello goes off. It's only when he goes out that we should see the impact of the quarrel on her. General note to Iago: "The American-ness of the character is not yet fully convincing. There is still a certain gentility about him which must go. Iago is there *to make a change* in the play and in society, and he wants to use Othello to make that change. His presence should always be disturbing."

MEMOS FROM MAROWITZ FOR IAGO
PURITAN BACKGROUND AS PLOY
Why is it that Iago's influence is so irresistible? Why is it that a man with Othello's clarity of mind is so susceptible to his Ancient's manipulations?

Othello is a black man successfully integrated into a white culture. In order to be so, he has accepted the fundamental tenets of that culture which, of course, include Christianity. He responds as a Christian up until his very last moment, when he reverts back to his original beliefs ("And say, besides, that in Aleppo once/Where a malignant and a turbanned Turk/Beat a Venetian and traduced the State"). We must assume that he was converted to Christianity and possesses the kind of zeal often found among Christian converts. To such a person, anyone who embodies Christian principles is holy and impressive since he himself is something of a newcomer to the faith. To perfect his own Christian behaviour, Othello willingly places himself into the hands of "professional" Christians. The disparity in rank between Othello and Iago is easily made up for by Iago's longer-standing in the faith.

To Othello, Iago represents these virtues in extremis. To Othello, Iago personifies the Moral Demeanour. Iago's façade is that of the sterling Puritan. He does not swear. While others (Cassio, Montano), are drunk, he is sober. He cannot bear to describe profane acts ("Lie . . . with her, on her, what-you-will . . ."). The merest suggestion of marital infidelity sends him into a repressed frenzy of moral admonishment, and it is this attitude which affects Othello. Perhaps Othello does not care ". . . if the General camp, Pioneers and all, had tasted her sweet body" so he had nothing known; but so long as Iago exerts his puritan influence on Othello, the General reacts in terms of Iago's moral outrage. For him, Desdemona is already damned and Cassio deserving of the worst punishment that can be meted out to him. The only power that a man like Othello could respect is moral power, and when confronted by that in the person of Iago, he is helpless before its sway.

It would be trite and pointless to play Iago as if he were simply a clever schemer and Othello a hopeless dupe. Everything we know of Othello defies that kind of interpretation, but if one plays Iago as a posing puritan, laying down a strict code of honour which is alien to the Moor but which he is obliged to accept, and whose strictness demands the highest punishment for transgression, there is a reasonable basis on which Iago's manipulation can become plausible. The problem with Iago is not to define his true character and why he behaves as he does: that is a donnée of the play and takes care of itself. No. The great problem is to define the character received by Othello, and to dope out a rationale for that mammoth deception.

NEW MOTIVATION FOR IAGO

For centuries, critics have agreed that, given the enormity of his crime, Iago lacks sufficient motivation. His claim of Emilia's infidelity with Othello is clearly implausible and, if he wanted merely to rise in rank, he needn't have exposed himself to all the dangers inherent in a murderous conspiracy. But if Othello is the epitome of the House Nigger (the conformist black) and Iago of the Field Nigger (the revolutionary black) then a legitimate motivation can be provided for Othello's destruction. Iago you might say is the last person to criticize, for he is a subversive, a liar and a cheat, but given the unshakeability of certain black totems in the white power-structure, the same criticism could be lodged against Eldrige Cleaver, Huey Newton or Malcolm X – all men with prison records and, in the eyes of white society, disreputable types. CM

Wednesday 17 May

Working on monologues. Charles gets the three actors – Brabantio, Desdemona and Iago – to perform them simultaneously, with great success. The exercise releases inhibitions and strengthens concentration. End the day with a run-through lasting one and three-quarter hours. Charles's reluctance to prune the text seems justified. Of the fifteen minutes shed since Saturday only about three are accounted for in cuts, the rest in general tightening up. Morale is visibly strengthened.

Charles congratulates the company and says that the problems which remain are more his than theirs. "The play doesn't hang together yet. Structurally it breaks in two, with Scene 9 as the dividing point. The first half is a series of comments on Shakespeare's *Othello*, the second half a story about a group of actors. This change isn't properly prepared for and makes for a rather broken-backed effect in consequence. The last scene now has a basic plausibility but there are still moments when it drops back into a straight rendering of the text."

"I started out right from the beginning working to make the most blatant contrast possible between all the kind of mother-fucking, shit, white-pussy type phrases that would come into Black American speech, so as to get the maximum conflict between that, the hip contemporary language, and traditional Shakespearian verse. Because one thing that began to emerge during the course of the writing was that there shouldn't be any one set style, nor should there be a simple combination of modern situations and classical situations. One was trying to say something about the black political conflict in America, one was trying to say something about the conception that people have of Shakespeare's character Othello, and how that related to contemporary political concerns. And one was also trying to say that the characters themselves from Shakespeare's play, as a result of being around for almost four hundred years, have now detached themselves from their original context, so they're in a sense roaming free in a kind of cultural terrain, and therefore they can be appropriated and put into a new context, although all the resonances from the original play will still be part of those characters. These three elements were what one tried to use, and, frankly, I think that was too ambitious. It created an enormous number of confusions which were not properly resolved in the play." CM

Robin brings in a new design for the set – scrapping the cage idea completely in favour of a complex structure of bars and chains to go on the upstage wall.

Thursday 18 May
Discuss Scene 9 in the light of yesterday's run. Charles: "The basis of Iago's criticism of Othello is that he's following whitey's script and solving the problem of his guilt in whitey's way. The play is asking, what is this black general doing at the head of a white army? But it's also questioning the different ways of playing Othello – for example the almost caricatured West Indian of Olivier's reading."
CHARLES: Why does Othello commit suicide?
RUDI: Because he's overcome with guilt at Desdemona's murder.
CHARLES: Why feel guilty? After all Othello has been the victim of a conspiracy of white officers to demote him and deprive him of his wife.

> *"This really is not Shakespeare's Othello, which is just a context into which one has written another play. The point of reference is the general conception that most people have of the play* Othello *by William Shakespeare, and, also, the general conception that people have of the character Othello, as a noble Moor. This was the starting-point for reversing people's expectations about the play, so that it couldn't really have been done with anything other than the original play in the background.*
>
> *The notion is that a black actor playing the character of Othello has a responsibility to* Othello's *implications, both in Shakespeare's play and in the contemporary world. If you are a black actor, and you're playing Othello, you have to ask questions like, why is this black man in this particular white situation? In other words, ask* political *questions about the old play. That seems to me a legitimate way of approaching contemporary political ideas through classical and traditional material in which those ideas were never intended to be in the first place, but in which they have evolved simply as a result of those plays still being around."* **CM**

New opening for Scene 9. Substitute "It is the cause" for "Had it pleased heaven To try me with affliction" as the soliloquy that Iago interrupts. It makes a more direct link into Scene 11. Try out various ways for Iago to distract Othello's attention – caricaturing him, interrupting, repeating the speech after him – but fail to find a satisfactory solution. It's not difficult for Iago to irritate Othello but it needs a way of doing this that is appropriate to the context. Decide to leave it for the time being. Iago, Cassio and Othello have got their costumes and rehearse in them for the rest of the day. Run the collage for speed. Elaborate several of the moves here away from naturalism into pirouettes, dance steps, or animal-like prowling.

Going on to the last scene. The actors are asked to speak their sub-text in the pauses. Desdemona's action in the first part of the scene: "I want to get him started." Charles: "She shouldn't just be playing bewilderment here. By not going through with his scene, Othello is violating his contract and the actress's loyalty goes instinctively to the management." Judy appeals silently to the prompt corner for help. The danger here is that she may just seem to be acting badly instead of being an actress acting badly because she's nervous. Work to achieve a balance between pantomimed anxiety in the pauses and a hysterical overplaying of the text.

Decide to cancel the extra performance on 3 June. Stuttgart aren't offering a large enough guarantee, and the financial risk involved is too great, particularly since it would mean paying for the company to stay in Germany in the interim.

Friday 19 May
Start the day with group exercises. Everyone standing in a semi-circle. The person on the left lays down a basic beat which is added to in turn by the others until a composite group sound is built up. The exercise is repeated using plosives instead of fully vocalized sounds, and as a last variation the actors are asked to use the names of diseases and find a movement which in some way corresponds to the particular malady they've chosen. It's an exercise both in concentration and ensemble playing. Each actor has to hang on to his own sound and movement and not be thrown by what other people are doing while at the same time making sure that his contribution is integrated into the rhythm built up by the group as a whole.

Regroup in a circle walking slowly round the room, with the person in front leading the others in a grotesque sound-and-movement. This speeds up gradually with one actor replacing another at the head of the line until the changes are happening at dizzying speed. Remarkable how quickly stiffness or self-consciousness disappear when there's no time left for conscious selection. The exercises are an ideal complement to Charles's usual rehearsal methods and bring a much needed ease and looseness to the playing.

Scene 1 Charles tells the Duke and Lodovico: "You're playing the situation as described in the language and not letting the language grow out of the situation." After lunch try on costumes and then run the play. Problem with the ropes in the storm scene, which are getting caught up in people's cloaks.

Charles has scripted some interjections for the opening of Scene 9 but it's still not right. Need to find something more positive to make the change from the end of Brabantio's comic monologue into the final section of the play. Working over Othello's speeches at the end of the day: some of them are beginning to go too fast for sense.

Saturday 20 May

Last day of *Hamlet* and *How Beautiful With Badges*. Meeting with Robin at 11.30 to discuss the set. What is eventually decided on for Wiesbaden is a distillation of the original concept – not a full cage with bars every 18 inches but just two bars (chains stretching from floor to ceiling) on each side. At the Open Space the acting area will be enclosed on four sides by crossed chains, shutting in the actors but not interfering with either the lighting or the sightlines. Decide to buy whatever chains will be needed for the Open Space, and take them with us to Wiesbaden.

At the Open Space in the afternoon, after working in outside rehearsal rooms. The collage is much more startling at such close quarters, but in general everything looks very cramped. Introduction to Scene 9 again. Charles: "We really need another scene here." Decide to stick with what we've got at the moment – scripted interjections from Iago – although this is much of a muchness with what has gone before. It'd be nice to find something completely new.

Going on to Scene 4. Othello and Iago are asked to play the scene from opposite sides of the auditorium. The action has been getting encrusted with fussy movement and gesture. This restores the clear line.

Sunday 21 May

Play out the collage using sounds to express the underlying sub-text.
"The object of the exercise is not just to make peculiar noises but to
provide an X-ray of what is going on beneath the surface." Anton
finds a series of insinuating little tunes for Iago that are particularly
expressive. Proceed to a full-scale sing-through of the scene. Charles:
"It's not just a question of vocalizing individual beats. It's an exercise in playing together. There are all sorts of possibilities here –
certain sections are trios, others quartets, others quintets and so on.
You should try and make all this clear." There's a certain amount of
giggling at first until people get used to the idea, but after a while
the exercise develops its own logic. The handkerchief scene is especially exciting – Rudi, heavy, accusing, with a dark-toned chromatic
spiritual; Anton egging him on in a light skittering staccato like a
sinister refugee from *The Barber of Seville*; and Judy protesting her
innocence in responses borrowed from the Church of England
liturgy.

Full run-through. A great stride forward, the company beginning
to phrase the play as a whole. It's no longer just an accumulation of
scenes, but is starting to acquire an overall shape. Having got *Hamlet*
and the Brenton play out of the way obviously makes a big difference. Scene 9 appears even more clearly as being the weak link.
Charles reblocks it to try and underline the relationships spatially.
Decided to start Scene 11 with a prompt from the stage manager,
establishing its tone unequivocally.

Monday 22 May

Drums arrive and are worked on. Reject drum sticks as being too
Sousa-like. Play out Scene 9 from completely different standpoint
now, with the characters behaving contrary to their true intentions.
Desdemona and Lodovico are in love with Iago, and although they
are trying to get him out of the play should attempt to convey to him
that they are really on his side. Othello is "a complete dumb-bell"
and Iago an upper-middle-class English civil servant trying to get
what he wants as quietly and as reasonably as possible.

In the evening, run the play before an invited audience, who are
asked to stay behind afterwards for discussion. Charles very anxious
to keep the cast out of the way for this. A try-out of *Sam Sam* in
similar circumstances had a disastrously destructive effect on morale.

A fairly mixed reaction, with everyone contradicting everyone else. Four main points emerge, however.

1. Desdemona's looking to prompt corner in the last scene is open to misconstruction. The audience doesn't get that she's wondering what the hell is going on. Looks too much as if something horrible is about to pounce on her from the wings.

2. Generally unclear whether the last scene is being played out by Shakespeare's characters or the actors performing them.

3. The transition in Scene 9 where the actors step out from behind their roles isn't properly established.

4. Someone complains that the collage is going too fast for comprehension. It's evidently still possible to mistake its dreamlike structure for straight exposition.

Tuesday 23 May

Charles gives notes on last night's run. "Iago can go further into relaxation and comedy. Having an audience will help here. The problem with the collage is that it's not real enough to be unreal. What makes it dreamlike is when each section is quite precise but there are no transitions between them. The whole thing is based on the removal of transitions and connecting links."

Discuss the cutting of Othello's throat. What Charles wants here is a knife that will squirt blood along the blade. The stage management have done some research and discover that there is only one such knife in London and that has been made specially for the National Theatre's production of *Richard II*. Decide to leave it till after Wiesbaden. In a proscenium theatre no one's going to be able to see it anyway. Press photo-call for Judy at 4.0.

There is another invited audience this evening, smaller this time. Rudi's stepping out of character in Scene 9, from noble Moor to broad West Indian, is properly shocking. The whole second half of the play is beginning to draw together, though Brabantio's monologue is now missing a little of its full effect by being too three-dimensional. The character Brabantio is getting in between the stand-up comic and his audience. Charles gives notes afterwards.

Wednesday 24 May

Fly to Germany.

Thursday 25 May

Technical walk-through in the Schauspielhaus from 10.30 to 2.30. Can't do the lighting today as it's still rigged for a performance of Handel's *Ariodante* at night. A German television crew in attendance to film the proceedings. Open the production out to hit the stage, which is considerably larger than our largest rehearsal room. Getting people on and off is a bit tricky. Entrances are made up two staircases set in the floor which prove difficult to negotiate in the dark. The stage is also steeply raked with a five-foot drop at the back. Hope to God no one falls off and breaks a limb. Greatly impressed by the efficiency and helpfulness of the stage crew who put up our set for us to rehearse on and then dismantle it again ready for the opera in the evening.

Friday 26 May

Arrive to start lighting at 8.30. Hang specials till 10.0 Lighting from 10.0 to 12.0, followed by technical dress-rehearsal with the actors. The storm scene doesn't look right lit from out front. Can't get the right disembodied quality. Solve this by mounting specials in the wings. Today's session is more rushed. We don't manage to get in a proper dress-rehearsal but have to make do with a stopping run. Charles reminds the cast to project like mad to fill this two-thousand-seater auditorium, and warns them, "Most of the audience won't understand English, let alone Negro slang. You've got to be prepared to face total blank incomprehension." Everyone rather apprehensive, remembering that Charles's last venture here – a production in German of Webster's *White Devil* – had been the subject of violent controversy and a number of people had walked out. In the event these fears prove groundless. All the jokes get across – suspect the audience contains a high proportion of American servicemen – and each blackout is greeted with a sound of applause. Press conference after the show. Charles says that he hadn't set out with the intention of writing any of the scenes himself, but it had proved impossible to get across the points he wanted simply by re-jigging the Shakespearian text.

Saturday 27 May

Call for notes at 6.30. Charles: "You can afford to let the audience come to you much more. All the energy that was being diffused last night should now be kept within you – within you as a group. Use that opening to really establish contact with the other actors. Feel each other, each other's presence." Second performance, equally well received. Eddie Phillips finds a new way of beginning Scene 8, which extracts maximum comic value out of his transformation from Venetian senator to doleful Jewish comic. He comes on as Shakespeare's Brabantio and only switches into his Fagin-like character when he starts to speak. It's a question of not undercutting the first lines of the speech by letting the audience see what is coming. The British Council throw a party for us after the performance.

Monday 29 May

Eleven o'clock call. Charles breaks into the mood of general euphoria. "We have all been living in a fool's paradise." He warns people not to go by the reactions of a generous and elated festival audience. The production is in fact far from ready. The sense of the play has been quite lost. If it opened in London in its present state it would be a disastrous failure.

Sit down and go through the play as at a first reading. It's a very valuable exercise to test the truth of the performance in this small room after playing it in a gigantic auditorium. Charles stops the actors repeatedly to point out false emphases. Charles to Rudi: "I don't want to bore you with history but when Stanislavsky played Othello he found the whole key to his performance in those three words. 'Blood, blood, blood'." Judy, used to acting for the camera, is asked to do her Scene 6 soliloquy with a piece of cloth held in front of her face.

Tuesday 30 May

Difficulty finding rehearsal space. Now that our performance is over other groups take priority. Attempt to rehearse the collage on a balcony overlooking the main street. Detailed work proves impossible under the circumstances. Charles asks the actors to run the scene saying the speeches and dancing the sub-text. In the end forced to abandon the rehearsal entirely. Turn it into a limbering session instead. Everyone standing around in circle. Without anyone consciously initiating the movement, the group converge on the centre with an animal sound-and-movement. Repeat this in reverse, again on a shared impulse. In the circle again, someone takes a sound-and-movement expressing some fictional character, carries it over to someone else who chooses another sound-and-movement and carries that on, and so on. Fly back to England.

Wednesday 31 May
While the company has been in Germany, the Open Space has been completely repainted from floor to ceiling. Desdemona's bed has been built, the lights hung, and the masking put up. All that remains to be done is to fit the chains that have been brought back from Wiesbaden on the plane. No rehearsals called. Spend the day lighting. Press photo-call at 4.0 p.m.

Thursday 1 June
Work through the play, restaging it to fit the Open Space. With the audience on three sides sightlines are quite a problem. The essential action has to be moved as far upstage as possible. Technical dress-rehearsal in the evening. Inevitably it's flat after the excitements of performing in public.

Friday 2 June
Two notes from last night: a lot of Othello's speeches are going too fast for sense, and Iago has lost a lot of his American-ness. Charles: "Lack of effort is a value here. We can't feel relaxed if you're working that hard – especially in somewhere as small as the Open Space."

Re-block Scene 1, which one of the German reviews has described as stiff and uninteresting.

The stage management have come up with their own home-grown version of the National's trick knife. The blood is kept in the knife's handle, which is hollow, and should pour down the blade when the stopper is unplugged. It seems simple enough in theory but in practice something goes wrong every time. The device is cut for to-night's run. We shall have to think again. The giant handkerchief which comes down from the roof works perfectly, however, despite Charles's initial doubts.

First preview. Everyone very tense, wondering how it will go down with an English audience. In the event, their performances have a nervous intensity that batters the audience into submission. The atmosphere is never as charged as this again, not even on the first night.

Saturday 3 June
Work through bits and pieces all afternoon. The only major change is in the collage, where Charles dims the lighting to make the orgy more suggestive. Spend time getting the wafting of the giant handkerchief right. Second preview. Very uneven performance. The good bits better than they've ever been and the bad bits worse. The chief gain this evening is that Judy and Rudi have cut the umbilical cord linking performance to rehearsal and thoroughly possessed their roles for the first time. The knife is now squirting blood all right but it still can't be seen. After the *pretended* deaths of Iago and Desdemona, it badly needs something sensational here.

Sunday 4th June
Call for notes at 6.30. Andrej Wajda who had seen the show last night got the impression that Iago in the last scene was part of the white conspiracy against Othello. Charles feels that to avoid this misunderstanding the distinction between Iago's "acted" death and "real" resurrection needs to be made much clearer. Third preview.

Monday 5 June
No performance. The Young Vic have announced that their new production of *The Alchemist* will have its first night on Thursday, the same day as our opening. Phone all the critics to remind them that we had booked that date several weeks ago. In the event most of them agree to come to us.

Tuesday 6 June
Everyone very refreshed after their day off. Introduce another change into the last scene, only this time with the aim of making it more, not less, ambiguous. Just before Othello is about to strangle her, Desdemona is directed to break from him in panic. It's now uncertain who it is he's murdering – the actress or the character. New solution to the knife problem. The blood is now squirted from a device concealed in Lodovico's signet ring. This is much more satisfactory. All the ambiguous nuances of the preceding scene are resolved by the unmistakable fact of there being blood all over everywhere. Fourth preview.

Wednesday 7 June

Fifth preview. Previews are normally the time when the nuances of
a particular production get straightened out. Here working on and
around a familiar text the nuances *are* the meaning. The traditional
first night remark, "It looks like a different play," takes on a new
resonance in the context.

Thursday 8 June

Call for notes at 5.30. Charles asks for more speed in the collage –
yesterday's run had been a bit sluggish. Charles: "The biggest
problem about tonight is that it is the first night. Everyone is going
to be involved in their own emotional state. I want you to make a
conscious effort to play together – play with the other people on
stage, and don't play your memories of what happened in Wiesbaden or at some rehearsal two weeks ago. In each scene there is a
point to make. Make it and go, there's nothing else to stick around
for. Don't linger. The watchword for tonight is touch – and go.
Touch – and go." It's the best performance yet. Afterwards everyone
is very relaxed and contented as if, in the end, it had been easier than
they'd expected. Tomorrow we start rehearsals for a new Sam
Shepard play *The Tooth of Crime*. Malcolm and David, who are
playing the two leading roles, are wondering how *that* will go.

SOME PRODUCTION COSTS

Set	£300
Costumes	£240
Rehearsal Space	£70
Rehearsal Salaries	£800
Design	£150
	£1,560

Rent of Open Space	£62 per week
Administrative Outgoings	£85 per week
Playing Salaries	£182 per week

Compiled by John Burgess